scrappy
QUILTS

Published by John Wiley & Sons, Inc., Hoboken, New Jersey
Published simultaneously in Canada

For general information about our other products and services, please contact our Customer Care Department within the United States at (800) 762-2974, outside the United States at (317) 572-3993 or fax (317) 572-4002.

Wiley also publishes its books in a variety of electronic formats. Some content that appears in print may not be available in electronic books. For more information about Wiley products, visit our web site at www.wiley.com.

ISBN 978-0-470-62623-8

Printed in the United States of America

10 9 8 7 6 5 4 3 2 1

Our Promise
Prior to publication we cut, sew, and assemble at least four blocks of every quilt to verify the accuracy of our patterns and instructions. Then an experienced team of editors reviews the materials lists, how-to directions, and illustrations to make sure the information we provide you is clear, concise, and complete.

Better Homes and Gardens®

Scrappy QUILTS

29 Favorite Projects from the Editors of
AMERICAN PATCHWORK & QUILTING®

WILEY

John Wiley & Sons, Inc.

CONTENTS

light & bright

rich & warm

modern makeover

welcome!

Fabric scraps are a natural by-product of a quilter's passion. With each rotary cut and snip through fresh yardage, you're bound to have bits, strips, and pieces leftover. But what do you do with that ever-growing stash? The answer is a scrappy quilt!

Chapter by chapter, you'll find quilts of all sizes organized by color inside this book. Is your pile filled with pastels or brights? Look through the Light & Bright chapter. How about deep jewel tones? Try the selection found in the Rich & Warm chapter. Or if your fabrics tend to have a more contemporary feel, look in the Modern Makeover chapter for inspiration. You'll find nearly 30 projects in all, many of which feature color options that show the quilts in entirely new color ways. With so many to choose from, you're bound to find just the right quilt so you can finally put those scraps to use.

Happy Quilting!

light & bright

circle upon circle

QUILT COLLECTOR **JULIE HENDRICKSEN**
PHOTOGRAPHER **ANDY LYONS**

Perfect for practicing curved piecing, this scrappy antique quilt features an Improved Nine-Patch block popular in the early 1930s, as well as a vibrant mix of colors and prints.

materials

- 37—¼-yard pieces assorted 1930s prints (blocks)
- ¾ yard solid blue (blocks)
- ½ yard solid light blue (blocks)
- ⅓ yard each solid green, solid peach, and solid pink (blocks)
- 1 yard solid yellow (blocks)
- 1⅛ yards solid orange (blocks)
- ¼ yard each solid purple and cream shirting (blocks)
- ⅞ yard solid red (blocks)
- 4⅓ yards muslin (blocks)
- ⅔ yard blue print (binding)
- 5 yards backing fabric
- 80×89" batting

Finished quilt: 73⅛×82⅝"

Quantities are for 44/45"-wide, 100% cotton fabrics.
Measurements include ¼" seam allowances. Sew with right sides together unless otherwise stated.

cut fabrics

Cut pieces in the order that follows. Make templates of patterns, which are on *Pattern Sheet 1*. (For details, see Make and Use Templates, *page 170*.) Be sure to transfer dots and center points marked on patterns to templates, then to fabric pieces. The dots are matching points and are used to join pieces.

From *each* 1930s print, cut:
▸ 2—3×42" strips
▸ 1—1¾×15" strip
From solid blue, cut:
▸ 5—1¾×42" strips
▸ 10—3×15" strips
From solid light blue, cut:
▸ 3—1¾×42" strips
▸ 6—3×15" strips
From *each* solid green, solid peach, and solid pink, cut:
▸ 2—1¾×42" strips
▸ 4—3×15" strips
From solid yellow, cut:
▸ 7—1¾×42" strips
▸ 14—3×15" strips
From solid orange, cut:
▸ 8—1¾×42" strips
▸ 16—3×15" strips
From *each* solid purple and cream shirting, cut:
▸ 1—1¾×42" strip
▸ 2—3×15" strips
From solid red, cut:
▸ 6—1¾×42" strips
▸ 12—3×15" strips
From muslin, cut:
▸ 542 of Pattern B
From blue print, cut:
▸ 1—21×42" rectangle, cutting it into enough 2½"-wide bias strips to total 350" in length for binding (For details, see Cutting Bias Strips, *page 174*.)

assemble centers

Color placement of the solid fabrics has been slightly modified from the original quilt so block centers can be strip-pieced in sets. The instructions that follow are for making a set of seven matching Improved Nine-Patch blocks using one 1930s print and solid blue.

[1] Sew together two 1930s print 3×42" strips and a solid blue 1¾×42" strip to make strip set A (**Diagram 1**). Press seams toward solid blue strip. Cut strip set into fourteen 3"-wide A segments.

[2] Sew together two solid blue 3×15" strips and a 1930s print 1¾×15" strip to make strip set B (**Diagram 2**). Press seams toward solid blue strips. Cut strip set into seven 1¾"-wide B segments.

[3] Sew together two A segments and one B segment to make a Nine-Patch unit (**Diagram 3**). Press seams toward A segments. The pieced unit should be 6¾" square including seam allowances. Repeat to make seven matching Nine-Patch units total.

[4] Placing the A template over each Nine-Patch unit, mark curved edges and transfer dots. Cut on marked lines to make seven blue Improved Nine-Patch blocks total (**Diagram 4**).

Note: To align the template accurately, Julie Hendricksen suggests cutting a window in the template the same size as the center square, then lining up the window with the square before marking.

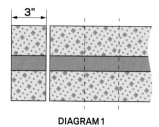

DIAGRAM 1

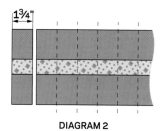

DIAGRAM 2

DIAGRAM 3

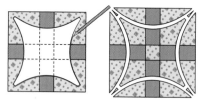

DIAGRAM 4

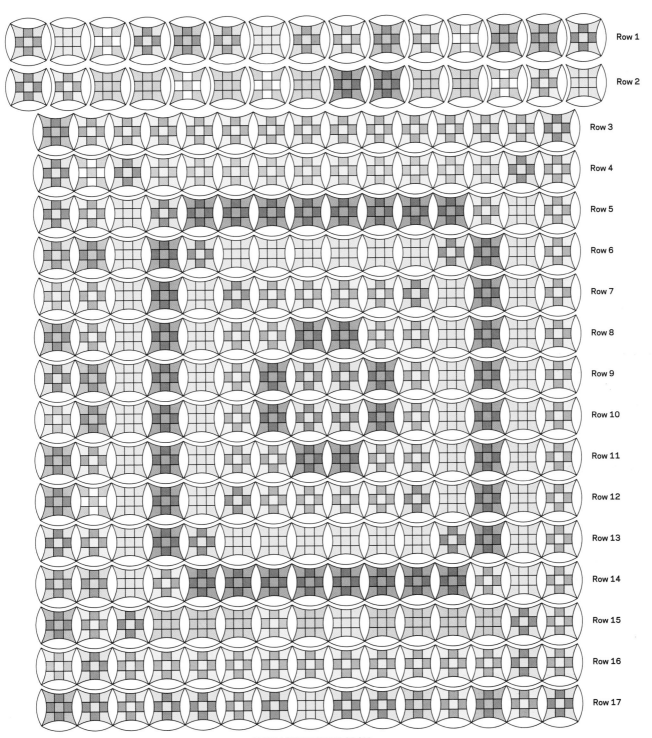

Row 1

Row 2

Row 3

Row 4

Row 5

Row 6

Row 7

Row 8

Row 9

Row 10

Row 11

Row 12

Row 13

Row 14

Row 15

Row 16

Row 17

QUILT ASSEMBLY DIAGRAM

[5] Using remaining 1930s print strips and solid purple or cream shirting strips, repeat steps 1 through 4 to make the following Improved Nine-Patch blocks: 35 of solid blue; 21 of solid light blue; 14 each of solid green, solid peach, and solid pink; 49 of solid yellow; 56 of solid orange; 7 each of solid purple and cream shirting; and 42 of solid red.

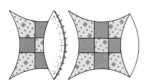

DIAGRAM 5   DIAGRAM 6

DIAGRAM 7   DIAGRAM 8

assemble quilt top

[1] Lay out Improved Nine-Patch blocks in rows (**Quilt Assembly Diagram**, *page 11*). You'll have four leftover blocks.

[2] When pleased with the arrangement, sew a muslin B piece to right-hand edge of the upper right-hand block.

To join curved edges, layer muslin B piece and block center, matching center marks on curved edges. Place a slender pin at center dots (**Diagram 5**). Then place a pin at each end of the sewing line. Continue pinning edges in between, picking up only a few threads at a time and easing the fabric until pieces fit together smoothly (**Diagram 6**).

Note: Pinning and sewing with the B piece on top will make it easier for you to maintain precise control of fabric pieces.

Sew together, removing each pin just before your needle comes to it; begin and end at ¼" seam allowance dots. Press seam toward block.

[3] Repeat Step 2 to add a muslin B piece to the block's top and bottom edges (**Diagram 7**). Press seams toward block.

[4] Add three muslin B pieces to 14 blocks total in Row 1 (**Quilt Assembly Diagram**). Sew four muslin B pieces to remaining block in Row 1.

❂ COLOR OPTION ❂

Make a table-mat version of Circle upon Circle using a three-by-three configuration of the shapes, which recalls the look of an old-fashioned game board.

By using a darker fabric in place of the muslin, the Nine-Patches recede and the black circles pop out to create a striking pattern.

ALTERNATE QUILT SIZES	WALL/LAP	FULL/QUEEN	KING
Number of Improved Nine-Patch blocks	144	360	484
Number of Pattern B pieces	312	758	1,012
Number of blocks wide by long	12×12	18×20	22×22
Finished size	58⅞" square	87⅜×96⅞"	106⅜" square
YARDAGE REQUIREMENTS			
Total of assorted 1930s prints	21—¼-yard pieces	52—¼-yard pieces	70—¼-yard pieces
Solid blue	½ yard	1⅛ yards	1⅜ yards
Solid light blue	¼ yard	⅝ yard	¾ yard
Yards each of solid green, solid peach, and solid pink	¼ yard	⅜ yard	½ yard
Solid yellow	⅝ yard	1 yard	1⅛ yards
Solid orange	¾ yard	1⅛ yards	1¼ yards
Yards each of solid purple and cream shirting	¼ yard	¼ yard	⅓ yard
Solid red	⅝ yard	⅞ yard	1⅛ yards
Muslin	2⅝ yards	6⅛ yards	8 yards
Blue print	⅝ yard	¾ yard	⅞ yard
Backing	3⅝ yards	7⅞ yards	9½ yards
Batting	65" square	94×103"	113" square

[5] In rows 2 through 17, add a muslin B piece to the right-hand and bottom edges of the blocks (**Diagram 8**). Sew three muslin B pieces to the remaining block in each row.

[6] Sew together pieces in each row; begin and end at ¼" seam allowance dots. Join rows to complete quilt top. Press seams toward block centers, pressing them open at seam intersections as necessary to reduce bulk.

finish quilt

[1] Layer quilt top, batting, and backing. (For details, see Complete the Quilt, *page 174*.)

[2] Quilt as desired. The antique quilt shown is outline-quilted ¼" from each seam. As a result, the design appears on the quilt back, giving a pleasing overall texture to the finished quilt.

[3] Use blue print binding strips to bind quilt. Since the quilt's edge is slightly scalloped, ease in a little extra binding along outside curves. At each inner corner of the scallops, the binding should form a small fold when it's turned over the edge to the back.

DESIGNER **AVIS SHIRER**
QUILTMAKER **JUDY SOHN**
QUILTER **LEANNE OLSON**
PHOTOGRAPHERS **SCOTT LITTLE**
AND **MARTY BALDWIN**

sweet lullaby

materials

- ½ yard *total* assorted light brown prints (Double Four-Patch blocks)
- 1⅔ yards *total* assorted cream prints (Double Four-Patch blocks, Sawtooth Star blocks, border)
- 1 yard *total* assorted light green prints (Sawtooth Star blocks, binding)
- ⅓ yard dark brown print
- 1⅜ yards backing fabric
- 41×49" batting

Finished quilt: 34½×42½"
Finished blocks: 4" square

Quantities are for 44/45"-wide, 100% cotton fabrics. Measurements include ¼" seam allowances. Sew with right sides together unless otherwise stated.

cut fabrics

Cut pieces in the following order.

From assorted light brown prints, cut:
- 6—1½×42" strips

From assorted cream prints, cut:
- 6—1½×42" strips
- 80—2½" squares (40 sets of 2 squares to match strips cut above)
- 160—1½×2½" rectangles (40 matching sets of 4 rectangles)
- 308—1½" squares (including 40 sets of 4 matching squares to match rectangles cut above)

From assorted light green prints, cut:
- 40—2½" squares
- 320—1½" squares (40 sets of 8 squares to match each 2½" square cut above)
- 4—2½×42" binding strips

From remaining light green prints, cut:
- 9—2½×21" binding strips or enough 2½"-wide strips to total 190" in length

From dark brown print, cut:
- 72—1½×2½" rectangles

Stars created with a gender-neutral mix of soft green prints are sprinkled among muted brown Irish Chains of Double Four-Patch blocks.

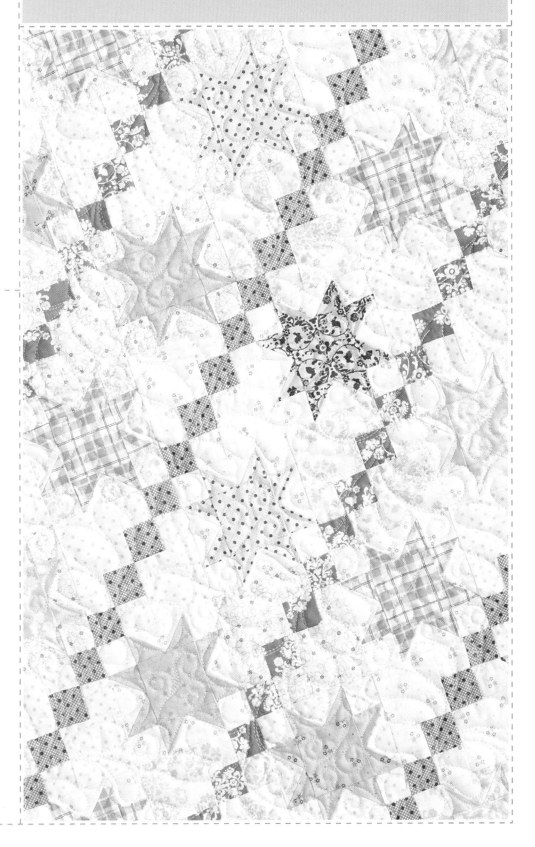

double four-patch blocks

[1] Join a light brown print 1½×42" strip and a cream print 1½×42" strip to make a strip set. Press seam toward light brown print strip. Repeat to make six strip sets total. Cut strip sets into 160—1½"-wide segments (Diagram 1).

[2] Join two segments to make a Four-Patch unit (Diagram 2). Press seam in one direction. The unit should be 2½" square including seam allowances. Repeat to make 80 Four-Patch units total.

[3] Referring to Diagram 3 for placement, sew together two Four-Patch units and two matching cream print 2½" squares in matching pairs. Press seams toward cream print squares. Join pairs to make a Double Four-Patch block. Press seams in one direction. The block should be 4½" square including seam allowances. Repeat to make 40 Double Four-Patch blocks total.

assemble sawtooth star blocks

[1] For one Sawtooth Star block, gather one 2½" square and eight 1½" squares from the same light green print; four 1½×2½" rectangles; and four 1½" squares from the same cream print.

[2] Use a pencil to mark a diagonal line on wrong side of each light green print 1½" square.

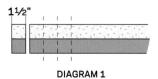

1½"

DIAGRAM 1

DIAGRAM 2

DIAGRAM 3

DIAGRAM 4

[3] Align a marked square with one end of a cream print 1½×2½" rectangle (Diagram 4; note direction of drawn line). Sew on marked line; trim seam allowance to ¼". Press open attached triangle.

[4] Align a marked square with opposite end of Step 3 rectangle (Diagram 4; again note direction of marked line). Stitch, trim, and press as before to make a Flying Geese unit. The unit should be 2½×1½" including seam allowances.

choosing fabrics: designer tips

▸ I usually start with a favorite piece of fabric, then add and subtract more fabrics until I like the overall look. At that point I walk away from the fabrics. If I still like my selections when I return, then it is a go! —AVIS SHIRER

▸ I begin by thinking about the scale of my blocks and the overall design. —AMY BUTLER

▸ I never start with just one fabric. I gather randomly from my stash (usually picking the fabric lying on top!). —ALICE BERG

▸ First I decide if I want a look that is warm, fun, young, winter, etc., then I decide on the colors. I find a focal point in the quilt design and choose that fabric first. —LAURA BOEHNKE

▸ Don't be afraid to try something new in terms of fabrics—embrace, play, and experiment. After all, a quilt is a piece of art. If it doesn't turn out the way you thought, there is always your next project! —CORI DERKSEN

▸ To me, a stunning large-print fabric begs to be a border of a quilt. I'll start with the border, then add fabrics for the blocks. —TAMMY JOHNSON

▸ The design is first for me. If it is more formal, then I want crisp contrast. If it is meant to be a cuddle-up quilt, then I want the fabrics to have less contrast. I almost always add brown to my quilts to warm them up. —CINDY BLACKBERG

[5] Repeat steps 3 and 4 to make four matching Flying Geese units total.

[6] Referring to **Diagram 5**, sew together the four matching cream print 1½" squares; four Flying Geese units; and light green print 2½" square in rows. Press seams away from Flying Geese units. Join rows to make Sawtooth Star block. Press seams in one direction. The block should be 4½" square including seam allowances.

DIAGRAM 5

[7] Repeat steps 1–6 to make 40 Sawtooth Star blocks total.

assemble quilt center

[1] Referring to **Quilt Assembly Diagram**, lay out Double Four-Patch blocks and Sawtooth Star blocks in 10 rows. Sew together blocks in each row. Press seams in one direction, alternating direction with each row.

[2] Join rows to make quilt center; press seams in one direction. The quilt center should be 32½×40½" including seam allowances.

assemble and add border

[1] Use a pencil to mark a diagonal line on wrong side of each remaining cream print 1½" square.

❈ COLOR OPTION ❈

The subdued stars and stripes featured in Sweet Lullaby come alive in this spirited rose, gold, and orange version.

Rather than muted browns for the Irish Chains, this quilt features a rose-colored chain strung among a single light tan tone-on-tone fabric. If you want a bigger or smaller version of this quilt, it's easy to modify the size by adding blocks to or subtracting blocks from each row.

[2] Referring to Assemble Sawtooth Star Blocks, steps 3 and 4, *page 16*, use brown print 1½×2½" rectangles and marked cream print squares to make 72 Flying Geese units.

[3] Referring to **Quilt Assembly Diagram**, sew together 16 Flying Geese units to make a short border strip. Press seams in one direction. The short border strip should be 1½×32½" including seam allowances. Repeat to make a second short border strip.

[4] Join two cream print 1½" squares and 20 Flying Geese units to make a long border strip (**Quilt Assembly Diagram**). Press seams in one direction. The long border strip should be 1½×42½" including seam allowances. Repeat to make a second long border strip.

[5] Sew short border strips to short edges of quilt center. Add long border strips to remaining edges to complete quilt top. Press seams toward border.

finish quilt

[1] Layer quilt top, batting, and backing; baste. (For details, see Complete the Quilt, *page 174.*)

[2] Quilt as desired.

[3] Bind with light green print binding strips. (For details, see Complete the Quilt.)

QUILT ASSEMBLY DIAGRAM

checkerboard charm

QUILT COLLECTOR **JULIE HENDRICKSEN**
PHOTOGRAPHER **GREG SCHEIDEMANN**

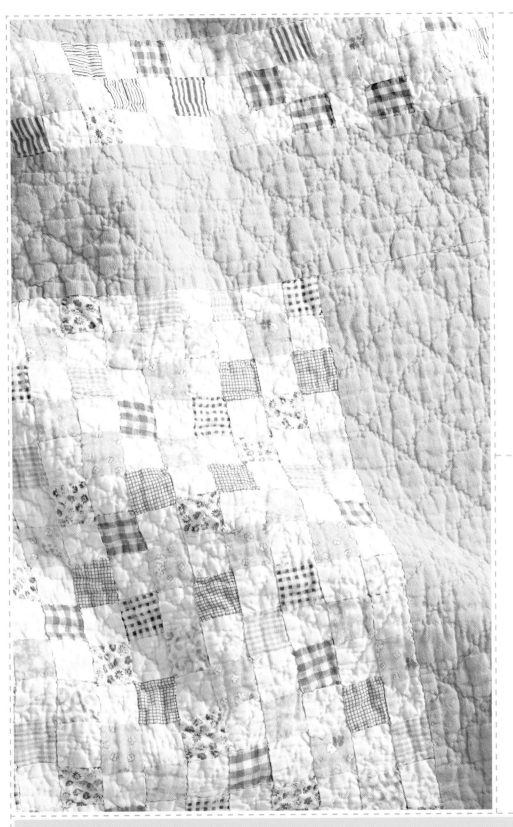

materials

- 15—18×22" pieces (fat quarters) assorted prints, checks, and stripes (blocks, middle border) For color proportions similar to the featured antique quilt, select fat quarters in the following breakdown: 4 pink, 3 yellow, 3 blue, 2 purple, 2 green, and 1 red.
- 3½ yards muslin (blocks, middle border)
- 4⅝ yards solid pink (sashing, inner and outer borders)
- ⅞ yard pink small check (binding)
- 8 yards backing fabric
- 96" square batting

Finished quilt: 89½" square
Finished block: 17" square

Quantities are for 44/45"-wide, 100% cotton fabrics. Measurements include ¼" seam allowances. Sew with right sides together unless otherwise stated.

cut fabrics

Cut pieces in the following order. Cut sashing, inner border, and outer border strips lengthwise (parallel to the selvages).

From assorted prints, checks, and stripes, cut:
- 145—1½×21" strips
- 36—1½" squares

From muslin, cut:
- 144—1½×21" strips
- 36—1½" squares

From solid pink, cut:
- 4—6½×91" outer border strips
- 4—4½×73" inner border strips
- 2—6½×63½" sashing strips
- 6—6½×17½" sashing rectangles

From pink small check, cut:
- 10—2½×42" binding strips

If you have an overflowing scrap basket, look to this striking antique quilt for inspiration. Speed up block assembly by strip-piecing those leftover fabric pieces together first.

assemble segments

Most blocks in this antique quilt are made of 17 rows of 17—1" squares each. However, some blocks have fewer squares, likely because they were trimmed off when the quiltmaker squared up her blocks.

To simplify construction, the following instructions call for all blocks to be pieced with the same number of squares.

[1] Referring to **Diagram 1**, sew together nine assorted print, check, and stripe 1½×21" strips and eight muslin 1½×21" strips to make strip set A. Press seams toward assorted prints. Repeat to make nine total of strip set A.

[2] Referring to **Diagram 1**, cut A strip sets into 105—1½"-wide A segments. (They should have a print square at each end.)

[3] Sew together nine muslin 1½×21" strips and eight assorted print, check, and

great gingham

From a distance it appears that the quilt's backing and binding fabrics are the same. A closer look reveals two different ginghams were used—a red and white for the backing and a pink and white for the binding.

stripe 1½×21" strips to make strip set B (Diagram 2). Press seams toward assorted prints. Repeat to make eight total of strip set B.

[4] Referring to **Diagram 2**, cut B strip sets into 96—1½"-wide B segments. (They should have a muslin square at each end.)

assemble blocks

Sew together nine A segments and eight B segments to make a block (Diagram 3). Press seams in one direction. The block should be 17½" square including seam allowances. Repeat to make nine blocks total. Set aside remaining segments for the middle border.

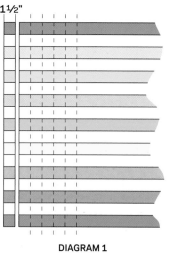

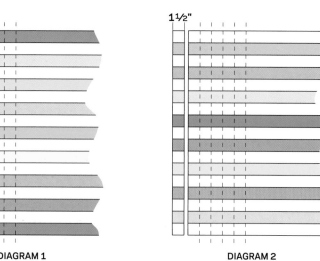

DIAGRAM 1

DIAGRAM 2

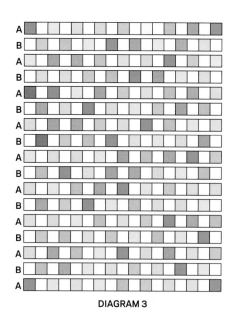

DIAGRAM 3

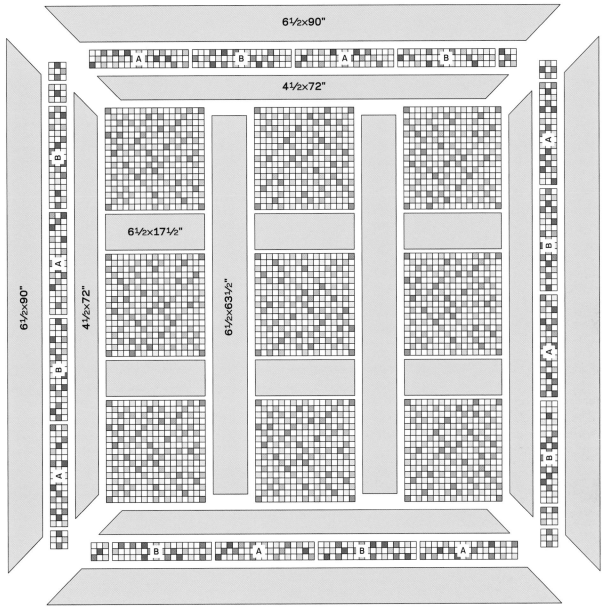

QUILT ASSEMBLY DIAGRAM

assemble quilt center

[1] Referring to **Quilt Assembly Diagram,** lay out blocks, sashing rectangles, and sashing strips in rows.

[2] Sew together blocks and sashing rectangles. Press seams toward sashing rectangles. Join block rows and sashing strips to make

quilt center. Press seams toward sashing strips. The quilt center should be 63½" square including seam allowances.

add inner border

[1] Aligning midpoints, sew inner border strips to opposite edges of quilt center, beginning and ending seams ¼" from quilt

center corners. Press seams toward border.

[2] Add remaining inner border strips to remaining edges of quilt center, mitering corners. (For details, see Mitering Borders, *page 173*.) Press seams toward border. The quilt center now should be 71½" square including seam allowances.

assemble and add middle border

In the featured quilt, three of the middle border corners are mitered and one is straight set. These instructions specify straight setting the corners in order to continue the checkerboard pattern.

[1] Referring to **Diagram 4**, join two remaining A segments and one remaining B segment to make Border Unit A. (It will have a print square in each corner.) Press seams toward A segments. Border Unit A should be 3½×17½" including seam allowances. Repeat to make eight total of Border Unit A.

[2] Referring to **Diagram 5**, sew together one A segment and two B segments to make Border Unit B. (It will have a muslin square in each corner.) Press seams toward A segment. Border Unit B should be 3½×17 ½" including seam allowances. Repeat to make eight total of Border Unit B.

[3] Referring to **Diagram 6**, sew together five assorted print, check, and stripe 1½" squares and four muslin 1½" squares in three rows. Press seams away from muslin squares. Join rows to make a dark Nine-Patch unit. Press seams away from center row. The dark Nine-Patch unit should be 3½" square including seam allowances. Repeat to make four dark Nine-Patch units total.

[4] Referring to **Diagram 7**, sew together five muslin 1½" squares and four assorted print, check, and stripe 1½" squares in three rows. Press seams away from muslin squares. Join rows to make a light Nine-Patch unit. Press seams toward center row. The light Nine-Patch unit should be 3½" square including seam allowances. Repeat to make four light Nine-Patch units total.

[5] Referring to **Quilt Assembly Diagram** on *page 23*, sew together two each of border units A and B. Add a dark Nine-Patch unit to the last Border Unit B to make a short middle border strip. Press all seams in one direction. The short middle border strip should be 3½×71½" including seam allowances. Repeat to make a second short middle border strip.

[6] Sew short middle border strips to opposite edges of quilt center. Press seams toward inner border.

[7] Referring to **Quilt Assembly Diagram** on *page 23*, lay out two light Nine-Patch units, two each of border units A and B, and one dark Nine-Patch unit in a row. Sew together pieces to make a long middle border strip. Press seams in one direction. The long middle border strip should be 3½×77½" including seam allowances. Repeat to make a second long middle border strip.

[8] Sew long middle border strips to remaining edges of quilt center. Press seams toward inner border.

[9] Aligning midpoints, sew outer border strips to opposite edges of quilt center, beginning and ending seams ¼" from quilt center corners. Add remaining outer border strips to remaining edges of quilt center, mitering corners, to complete quilt top. (For details, see Mitering Borders.) Press all seams toward outer border.

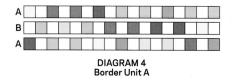

DIAGRAM 4
Border Unit A

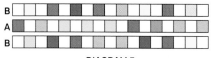

DIAGRAM 5
Border Unit B

DIAGRAM 6   **DIAGRAM 7**

QUILTING DIAGRAM

finish quilt

[**1**] Layer quilt top, batting, and backing; baste. (For details, see Complete the Quilt, *page 174*.)

[**2**] Quilt as desired. This antique quilt was hand-quilted in an allover diagonal grid through the center of each muslin square in the blocks, with the grid continuing into the borders.

[**3**] Bind with pink small check binding strips. (For details, see Complete the Quilt.)

REDHOTS

DESIGNER **MONIQUE DILLARD**   QUILTER **LEANNE OLSON**
PHOTOGRAPHER **KATHRYN GAMBLE**

Flying Geese and hourglass units in 24 red hues ranging from tomato to burgundy pair with 16 light prints for an ultrascrappy take on the classic two-color quilt.

materials

- 16—18×22" pieces (fat quarters) assorted cream prints (blocks)
- 24—18×22" pieces (fat quarters) assorted red prints (blocks, border, binding)
- 3¾ yards backing fabric
- 67×83" batting

Finished quilt: 60½×76½"
Finished block: 16" square

Quantities are for 44/45"-wide, 100% cotton fabrics. Measurements include ¼" seam allowances. Sew with right sides together unless otherwise stated.

cut fabrics

Cut pieces in the following order. See **Cutting Diagram**, on *page 28*, to get the most pieces from each fat quarter.

For her Flying Geese units, designer Monique Dillard makes oversize units, then trims them to size with her Fit to be Geese ruler. If using this ruler, don't cut 2½×4½" rectangles or 2½" squares. Follow manufacturer's instructions for cutting, piecing, and squaring up Flying Geese units.

From *each* cream print fat quarter, cut:
- 3—5¼" squares
- 6—2½×4½" rectangles
- 12—2½" squares

From *each* red print fat quarter, cut:
- 1—6½×21" rectangle for outer border
- 1—2½×15" binding strip
- 2—5¼" squares
- 4—2½×4½" rectangles
- 8—2½" squares

assemble flying geese units

[1] Use a pencil to mark a diagonal line on wrong side of each cream print and red print 2½" square.

[2] Align a marked cream print square with one end of a red print 2½×4½" rectangle (Diagram 1; note direction of drawn line). Sew on marked line; trim seam allowance to ¼". Press open attached triangle. Align a matching marked cream print square with opposite end of same rectangle (Diagram 1). Stitch, trim, and press as before to make a red Flying Geese unit. The unit should be 4½×2½" including seam allowances.

[3] Repeat Step 2 to make 96 red Flying Geese units total.

[4] Using marked red print 2½" squares and cream print 2½×4½" rectangles, repeat Step 2 to make 96 cream Flying Geese units (Diagram 2).

assemble hourglass units

[1] Use a pencil to mark a diagonal line on wrong side of each cream print 5¼" square.

[2] Layer a marked cream print 5¼" square atop a red print 5¼" square. Sew together with two seams, stitching ¼" on each side of drawn line (Diagram 3). Cut joined squares apart on drawn line to make two triangle units. Press each triangle unit open, pressing seam toward red print, to make two triangle-squares. Each should be 4⅞" square including seam allowances. Repeat to make 96 triangle-squares total.

[3] Use a pencil to mark a diagonal line perpendicular to the seam line on wrong side of 48 triangle-squares.

[4] Layer a marked triangle-square atop an unmarked triangle-square that is composed of different prints, placing cream print triangle atop red print triangle (Diagram 4).

[5] Sew pair together with two seams, stitching ¼" on each side of drawn line. Cut apart on drawn line to make two hourglass units (Diagram 4).

Press each unit open, pressing seam in one direction. Each hourglass unit should be 4½" square including seam allowances.

[6] Repeat steps 4 and 5 to make 96 hourglass units total.

assemble blocks

[1] Sew together two red Flying Geese units to make a red Flying Geese pair (Diagram 5). Press seam in one direction. The Flying Geese pair should be 4½" square including seam allowances.

DIAGRAM 1

DIAGRAM 2

DIAGRAM 3

DIAGRAM 4

DIAGRAM 5

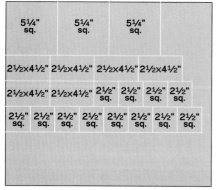

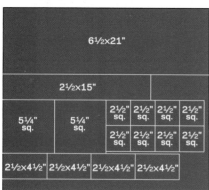

CUTTING DIAGRAM

DIAGRAM 6

DIAGRAM 7

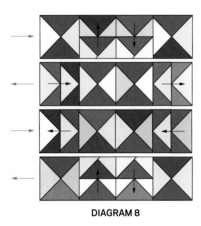

DIAGRAM 8

[2] Repeat Step 1 to make 48 red Flying Geese pairs total. So seams will abut in finished block, press seams toward top of 24 Flying Geese pairs and toward bottom of 24 pairs (Diagram 6).

[3] Using cream Flying Geese units, repeat steps 1 and 2 to make and press 48 cream Flying Geese pairs (Diagram 7).

[4] Referring to **Diagram 8**, lay out eight hourglass units, four red Flying Geese pairs, and four cream Flying Geese pairs in four rows (note direction of black arrows for placement of pairs). Sew together pieces in each row. Press seams in directions indicated by red arrows in diagram. Join rows to make an A block; press seams toward top of block. The block should be 16½" square including seam allowances. Repeat to make six A blocks total.

[5] Repeat Step 4, pressing seams toward bottom of block, to make a B block. Repeat to make six B blocks total.

assemble quilt center

[1] Referring to **Quilt Assembly Diagram,** lay out blocks in four rows, alternating blocks A and B. Sew together blocks in each row. Press seams in one direction, alternating the direction with each row.

[2] Join rows to make quilt center. Press seams in one direction. The quilt center should be 48½×64½" including seam allowances.

☼ COLOR OPTION ☼

Modify the size and number of colors to create a table runner. This version consists of three quilt blocks and five colors, and is framed by a 4¾"-wide, rather than the original 6½"-wide border. The multicolor palette creates an all-purpose runner to decorate the table throughout the year.

assemble and add border

[**1**] Cut assorted red print 6½×21" rectangles into lengths ranging from 8" to 18", then piece rectangles and trim lengths to make:
  ‣ 2—6½×64½" border strips
  ‣ 2—6½×60½" border strips

[**2**] Sew long border strips to long edges of quilt center. Add short border strips to remaining edges to complete quilt top. Press all seams toward border.

finish quilt

[**1**] Layer quilt top, batting, and backing; baste. (For details, see Complete the Quilt, *page 174*.)

[**2**] Quilt as desired. This quilt features an allover feather pattern across the quilt center and different feather designs in each border rectangle (**Quilting Diagram**).

6½×60½"

6½×64½"

QUILT ASSEMBLY DIAGRAM

QUILTING DIAGRAM

[**3**] Using diagonal seams, join assorted red print 2½×15" strips to make one long binding strip. Bind with pieced binding strip. (For details, see Complete the Quilt.)

mixed
bouquet

DESIGNER **MABETH OXENREIDER**   PHOTOGRAPHER **KATHRYN GAMBLE**

materials

- 3⅞ yards solid white (blocks, sashing, inner and outer borders)
- 10—18×22" pieces (fat quarters) assorted 1930s prints in blue, green, pink, and purple (blocks)
- 8—9×22" pieces (fat eighths) assorted solids in purple, green, blue, pink, and peach (blocks)
- ¾ yard solid gray-blue (blocks, middle border)
- ½ yard solid yellow (blocks, middle border)
- ¾ yard solid blue (blocks, binding)
- 4⅞ yards backing fabric
- 74×86" batting

Finished quilt: 68×80"
Finished blocks: 10" square

Quantities are for 44/45"-wide, 100% cotton fabrics. Measurements include ¼" seam allowances. Sew with right sides together unless otherwise stated.

cut fabrics

Cut pieces in the following order. Patterns are on *Pattern Sheet 1*. To make templates of the patterns, see Make and Use Templates, *page 170*. Be sure to transfer the dots to the templates, then to the fabric pieces. The dots are matching points and are necessary when joining the pieces.

Combine rotary cutting and templates for quick, accurate pieces. Rotary-cut strips in specified lengths from assorted prints, then use the templates to cut pieces from the strips (Cutting Diagram *on page 34*).

From solid white, cut:

- 8—6¼×42" strips for outer border
- 15—2½×42" strips for sashing and inner border
- 480 of Pattern A or 240—2¼" squares, cutting each in half diagonally for 480 A triangles total

Solids and prints play off each other in this reproduction-fabrics throw, which showcases a new interpretation of the Chrysanthemum block. The crisp white background directs attention straight to the angular blocks.

From *each* assorted 1930s print, cut:

▸ 6—1½×22" strips, cutting strips into a total of 8 each of patterns B, B reversed, and D

From *each* assorted solid fat eighth, cut:

▸ 4—1½×22" strips, cutting strips into a total of 8 each of patterns C and C reversed

From solid gray-blue, cut:

▸ 13—1½×42" strips for middle border

▸ 1—1½×42" strip, cutting it into 4 each of patterns C and C reversed

From solid yellow, cut:

▸ 7—1½×42" strips for middle border

▸ 2—1½×42" strips, cutting strips into a total of 8 each of patterns C and C reversed

From solid blue, cut:

▸ 8—2½×42" binding strips

▸ 1—1½×42" strip, cutting it into 4 each of patterns C and C reversed

From scraps of all solids, cut:

▸ 20—1½" squares

assemble blocks

[1] For one block gather 24 solid white A triangles; one set of four matching 1930s print B, B reversed, and D pieces; one set of four matching solid C and C reversed pieces; and one solid 1½" square.

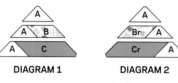

DIAGRAM 1   DIAGRAM 2

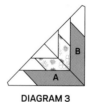

DIAGRAM 3

DIAGRAM 4

DIAGRAM 5

[2] Referring to **Diagram 1** for placement, lay out three solid white A triangles, one 1930s print B piece, and one solid C piece in three rows. Sew together pieces in each row. Press seams toward white triangles. Join rows to make subunit A. Press seams open. Repeat to make four total of subunit A.

[3] Referring to **Diagram 2** for placement, lay out three solid white A triangles, one 1930s print B reversed piece, and one solid C reversed piece in three rows. Sew together pieces in each row. Press seams toward white triangles. Join rows to make subunit B. Press seams open. Repeat to make four total of subunit B.

[4] Sew together one each of subunits A and B to make a quarter star unit (**Diagram 3**). Press seam open. Repeat to make four quarter star units total.

[5] Add two 1930s print D pieces to opposite edges of a solid 1½" square to make subunit C (**Diagram 4**). Press seams toward D pieces.

[6] Referring to **Diagram 5**, lay out the remaining 1930s print D pieces, quarter star units, and subunit C in three rows. Join pieces in each row. Press seams toward D pieces. Join rows to make a Chrysanthemum block. Press seams toward subunit C. The block should be 10½" square including seam allowances.

[7] Repeat steps 1–6 to make 20 blocks total.

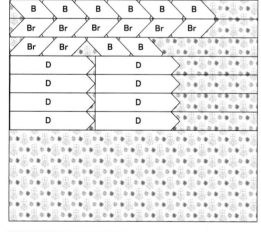

CUTTING DIAGRAM

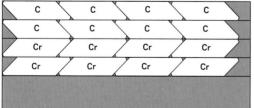

assemble quilt center and add inner border

[1] Cut and piece solid white 2½×42" strips to make:
- 3—2½×58½" sashing strips
- 2—2½×58½" inner border strips
- 2—2½×50½" inner border strips
- 16—2½×10½" sashing rectangles

[2] Referring to **Quilt Assembly Diagram**, sew together Chrysanthemum blocks and solid white 2½×10½" sashing rectangles in vertical rows. Press seams toward sashing.

[3] Join rows and solid white 2½×58½" sashing strips to make quilt center. Press seams toward sashing strips. The quilt center should be 46½×58½" including seam allowances.

[4] Sew solid white 2½×58½" inner border strips to long edges of quilt center. Add solid white 2½×50½" inner border strips to remaining edges. Press all seams toward border. The quilt center now should be 50½×62½" including seam allowances.

assemble and add remaining borders

[1] Cut and piece solid gray-blue 1½×42" strips to make:
- 4—1½×71" strips
- 4—1½×59" strips

[2] Cut and piece solid yellow 1½×42" strips to make:
- 2—1½×71" strips
- 2—1½×59" strips

[3] Referring to the **Quilt Assembly Diagram**, sew two gray-blue 1½×59" strips to a solid yellow 1½×59" strip to make a top border unit. Press seams toward gray-blue strips. Repeat to make a bottom border unit.

[4] Sew two gray-blue 1½×71" strips to a solid yellow 1½×71" strip to make a side border unit. Press seams toward solid yellow strip. Repeat to make a second side border unit.

[5] Aligning midpoints, sew side border units to long edges of quilt center, beginning and ending seams ¼" from corners of the quilt center. In the same manner, sew top and bottom border units to remaining edges, mitering corners. (For details, see Mitering Borders, *page 173*.) Press all seams toward middle border units. The quilt center now should be 56½×68½" including seam allowances.

[6] Cut and piece solid white 6¼×42" strips to make:
- 2—6¼×68½" outer border strips
- 2—6¼×68" outer border strips

[7] Sew solid white 6¼×68½" outer border strips to long edges of quilt center. Add solid white 6¼×68" outer border strips to remaining edges to complete quilt top. Press all seams toward middle border.

finish quilt

[1] Layer quilt top, batting, and backing; baste. (For details, see Complete the Quilt, *page 174*.)

[2] Quilt as desired. Designer Mabeth Oxenreider machine-quilted ¼" inside most seams in the blocks and sashing (**Quilting Diagram**). She also stitched in the ditch in the inner border and created 1"-wide parallel lines in the outer border.

[3] Bind with solid blue binding strips. (For details, see Complete the Quilt.)

QUILTING DIAGRAM

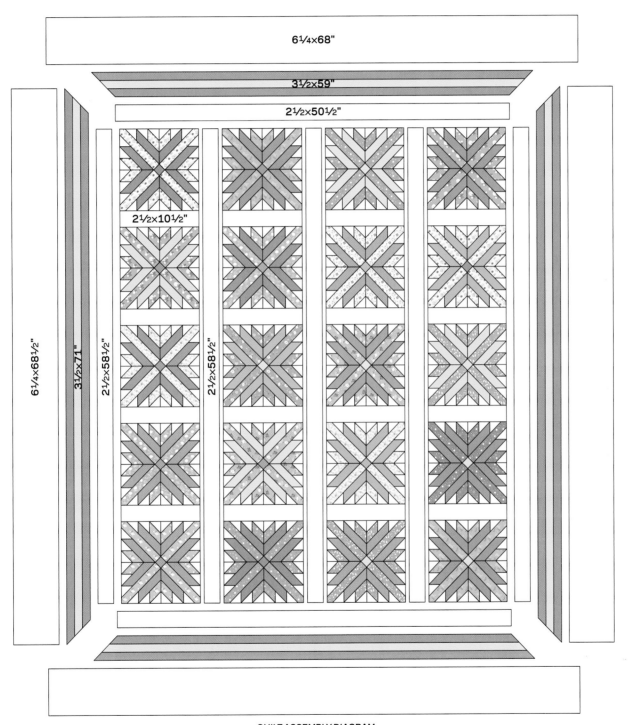

QUILT ASSEMBLY DIAGRAM

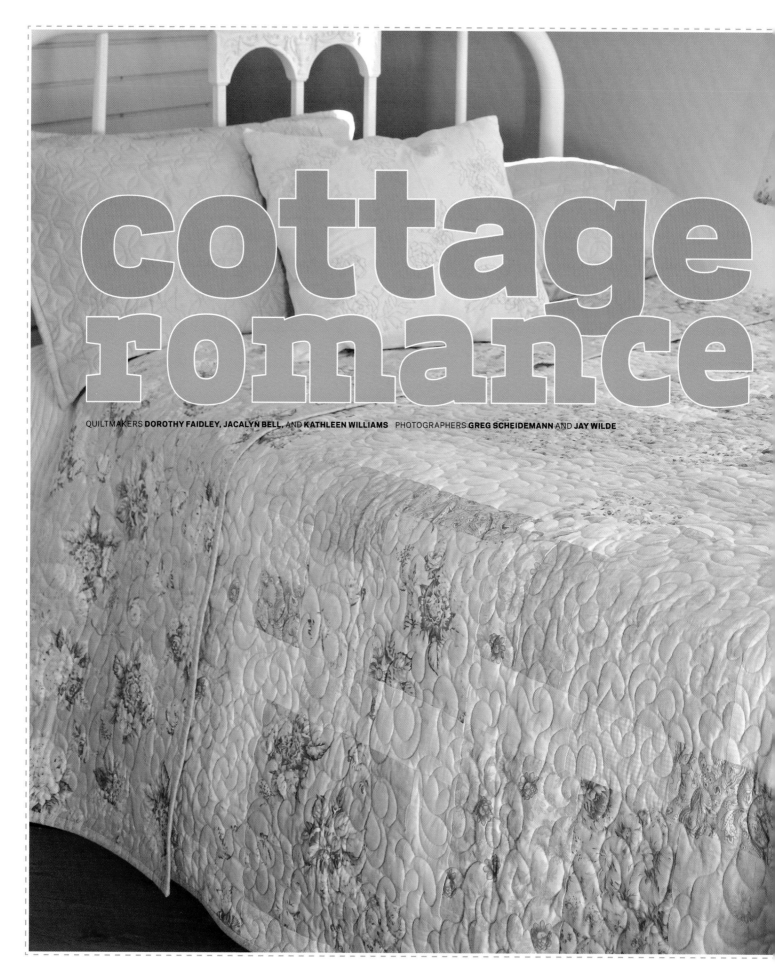

cottage romance

QUILTMAKERS **DOROTHY FAIDLEY, JACALYN BELL,** AND **KATHLEEN WILLIAMS**   PHOTOGRAPHERS **GREG SCHEIDEMANN** AND **JAY WILDE**

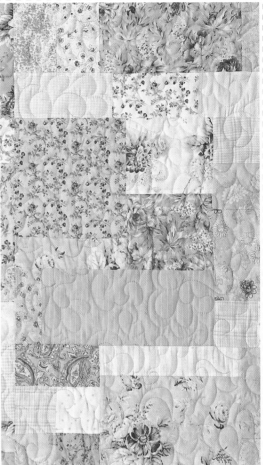

Combine easy piecing and a scrappy mix of soft florals and pretty pastels to make a romantic bed quilt.

materials

- 8¼ yards total assorted pastel yellow, pink, green, and white florals, plaids, and prints (blocks)
- ⅞ yard green print (binding)
- 8¼ yards backing fabric
- 97×107" batting

Finished quilt: 90½×100½"
Finished block: 15×20"

Quantities are for 44/45"-wide, 100% cotton fabrics.
Measurements include a ¼" seam allowance. Sew with right sides together unless otherwise stated.

cut fabrics

To make the best use of your fabrics, cut pieces in the following order.

From assorted pastel florals, plaids, and prints, cut:
- 15—10½" squares
- 15—8½" squares
- 15—6½" squares
- 15—5½×12½" rectangles
- 30—5½×6½" rectangles
- 30—4½×6½" rectangles
- 30—3½×7½" rectangles
- 60—3½×6½" rectangles
- 30—3½×4½" rectangles
- 60—3½" squares
- 15—2½×10½" rectangles
- 15—2½×8½" rectangles
- 15—2½×6½" rectangles
- 15—2½×5½" rectangles

From green print, cut:
- 10—2½×42" binding strips

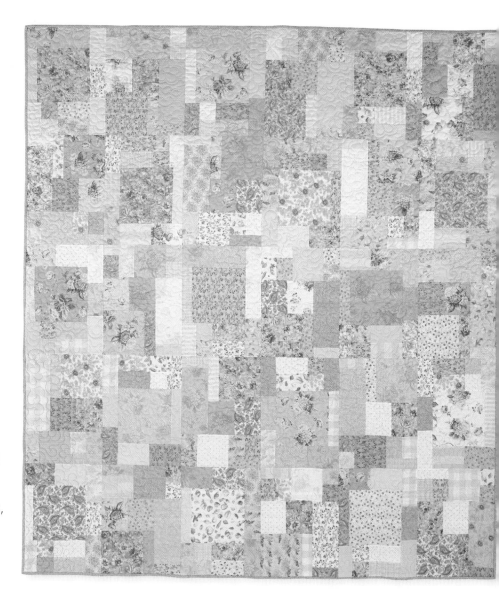

assemble block A

[1] Lay out the following assorted pastel floral, plaid, and print pieces: one 8½" square, one 6½" square, two 3½" squares, one 5½×12½" rectangle, one 2½×8½" rectangle, two 5½×6½" rectangles, one 2½×6½" rectangle, one 2½×5½" rectangle, and two 3½×4½" rectangles **(Diagram 1)**.

[2] Sew together pieces in each section. Press seams toward darker print. Then join sections to make a Block A. Press seams in one direction. Block A should be 15½×20½" including seam allowances.

[3] Repeat steps 1 and 2 to make 15 total of Block A.

assemble block B

[1] Lay out the following assorted pastel floral, plaid, and print pieces: one 10½" square, two 3½" squares, one 2½×10½" rectangle, two 3½×7½" rectangles, two 4½×6½" rectangles, and four 3½×6½" rectangles **(Diagram 2)**.

[2] Sew together pieces in each section. Press seams toward darker print. Then join sections to make a Block B. Press seams in one direction. Block B should be 15½×20½" including seam allowances.

[3] Repeat steps 1 and 2 to make 15 total of Block B.

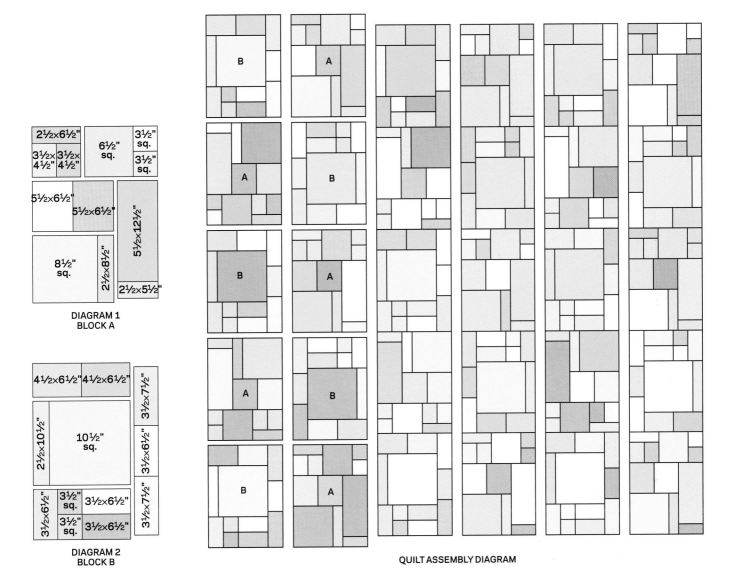

DIAGRAM 1
BLOCK A

DIAGRAM 2
BLOCK B

QUILT ASSEMBLY DIAGRAM

assemble quilt top

[1] Referring to **Quilt Assembly Diagram**, lay out blocks in six vertical rows, alternating blocks A and B.

[2] Sew together blocks in each row. Press seams toward B blocks. Join rows to complete quilt top. Press seams in one direction.

finish quilt

[1] Layer quilt top, batting, and backing; baste. (For details, see Complete the Quilt, *page 174*.)

[2] Quilt as desired. The featured quilt was machine-quilted with an allover flower design.

[3] Bind with green print binding strips. (For details, see Complete the Quilt.)

SCRAP basket

DESIGNER **SANDY KLOP** QUILTER **DIANA JOHNSON** PHOTOGRAPHER **GREG SCHEIDEMANN**

materials

- 2 yards total assorted medium and dark prints in green, blue, red, yellow, and brown (blocks, inner border)
- ⅛ yard *each* of cream basket print and cream floral (blocks)
- ½ yard cream dot (blocks)
- 4¾ yards mottled cream (blocks, setting and corner triangles, inner and outer borders)
- ⅞ yard gold basket print (blocks)
- ⅔ yard blue plaid (binding)
- 4⅝ yards backing fabric
- 83" square batting

Finished quilt: 76½" square
Finished block: 10" square

Quantities are for 44/45"-wide, 100% cotton fabrics. Measurements include ¼" seam allowances. Sew with right sides together unless otherwise stated.

cut fabrics

Cut pieces in the following order.

From assorted medium and dark prints, cut:

- 80—4⅛" squares, cutting each diagonally twice in an X for 320 small triangles total for inner border (*Note:* grain line is different than small triangles cut next)
- 128—2⅞" squares, cutting each in half diagonally for 256 small triangles total for blocks

From cream basket print and cream floral, cut:

- 28—2⅞" squares, cutting each in half diagonally for 56 small triangles total

Mix and match fabric scraps in the triangle-squares filling these piled-high baskets. A light background of cream setting squares and triangles adds to the lighthearted look.

From cream dot, cut:
- 6—2½×6½" rectangles
- 2—4⅞" squares, cutting each in half diagonally for 4 medium triangles total (you will use 3)
- 28—2⅞" squares, cutting each in half diagonally for 56 small triangles total

From mottled cream, cut:
- 8—4½×42" strips for outer border
- 3—15½" squares, cutting each diagonally twice in an X for 12 setting triangles total
- 9—10½" setting squares
- 2—8" squares, cutting each in half diagonally for 4 corner triangles total
- 26—2½×6½" rectangles
- 4—6¼" squares
- 7—4⅞" squares, cutting each in half diagonally for 14 medium triangles total (you will use 13)
- 40—4⅛" squares, cutting each diagonally twice in an X for 160 small triangles total
- 160—2⅜" squares, cutting each in half diagonally for 320 extra-small triangles total

From gold basket print, cut:
If using featured basket print, cut these squares on the bias so the basket print runs horizontally across the finished basket units.)
- 8—6⅞" squares, cutting each in half diagonally for 16 large triangles total
- 16—2⅞" squares, cutting each in half diagonally for 32 small triangles total

From blue plaid, cut:
- 8—2½×42" binding strips

assemble triangle-squares for blocks

[1] Sew together a cream basket print, cream dot, or cream floral small triangle and a medium or dark print small triangle to make a light triangle-square (Diagram 1). The triangle-square should be 2½" square including seam allowances.

[2] Repeat Step 1 to make 112 light triangle-squares total.

[3] Using two medium or dark print small triangles, repeat Step 1 to make 48 dark triangle-squares total (Diagram 2).

assemble blocks

[1] Referring to Diagram 3, lay out seven light triangle-squares, three dark triangle-squares, and three assorted medium or dark print small triangles in four rows. Sew together pieces in each row. Press seams in one direction, alternating direction with each row. Join rows to make a basket top. Press seams in one direction. Repeat to make 16 basket tops total.

[2] Sew together a gold basket print large triangle and a basket top to make a basket unit (Diagram 4). Press seam toward gold basket print. The basket unit should be 8½" square including seam allowances. Repeat to make 16 basket units total.

[3] Referring to Diagram 5, sew a gold basket print small triangle to one end of a mottled cream 2½×6½" rectangle to make a basket side. Press seam toward triangle. Repeat with a second gold basket print small triangle and a second mottled cream 2½×6½" rectangle, sewing triangle to opposite end of rectangle, to make a mirror-image basket side (Diagram 5).

DIAGRAM 1   DIAGRAM 2

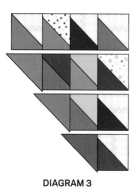

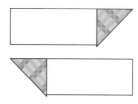

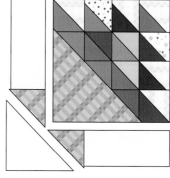

DIAGRAM 3   DIAGRAM 4   DIAGRAM 5   DIAGRAM 6

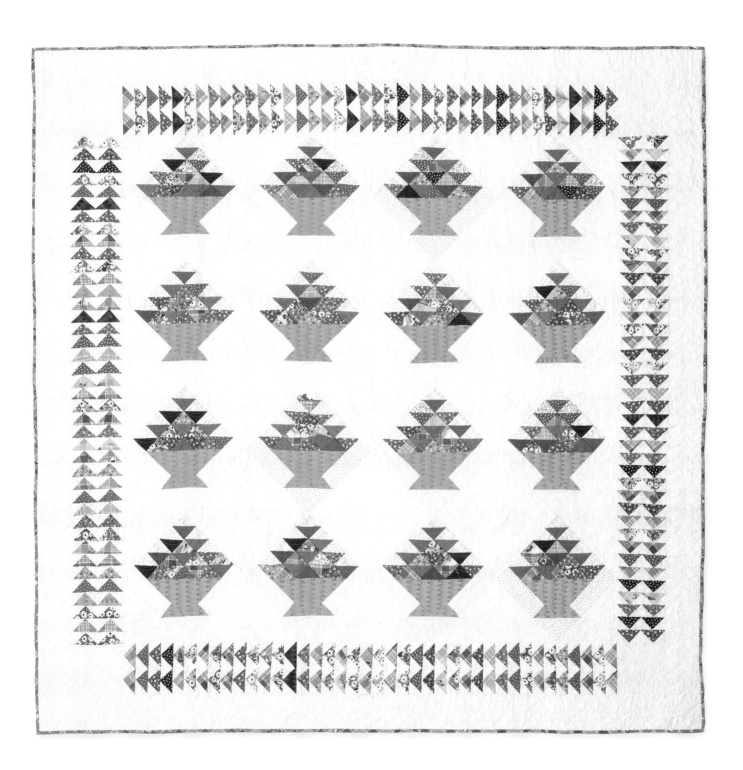

[4] Join basket sides to adjacent edges of a basket unit (Diagram 6). Press seams toward basket sides. Sew a mottled cream medium triangle to bottom edge of basket unit to make a block. Press seam toward mottled cream. The block should be 10½" square including seam allowances.

[5] Repeat steps 3 and 4 to make 16 blocks total, substituting six cream dot 2½×6½" rectangles and three cream dot medium triangles in three of the blocks.

assemble quilt center

[1] Referring to **Quilt Assembly Diagram,** lay out blocks and mottled cream setting squares and setting triangles in seven diagonal rows.

[2] Sew together pieces in each row. Press seams toward setting squares and triangles. Join rows; press seams in one direction.

[3] Add mottled cream corner triangles to complete quilt center. Press seams toward corner triangles. The quilt center should be 57" square including seam allowances.

assemble and add inner border

For precise piecing of the border segments, you may prefer paper piecing instead of traditional piecing. See *Pattern Sheet 1* for the Border Paper-Piecing Pattern.

[1] For one border segment, gather two matching medium or dark print small triangles, one mottled cream small triangle, and two mottled cream extra-small triangles. Sew medium or dark print small triangles to short edges of a mottled cream

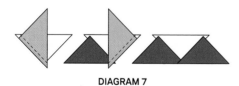

DIAGRAM 7

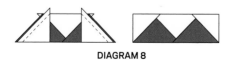

DIAGRAM 8

small triangle, offsetting points by ⅜" (Diagram 7). Press seams toward darker triangles.

[2] Join mottled cream extra-small triangles to ends of Step 1 unit to make a border segment **(Diagram 8).** Press seams toward darker triangles. If necessary, trim the extra-small triangles' dog ears. The border segment should be 6¼" long including seam allowances.

[3] Repeat steps 1 and 2 to make 160 border segments total.

[4] Referring to **Quilt Assembly Diagram,** sew together 40 border segments to make an inner border strip. Press seams in one direction. The strip should be 6¼×57" including seam allowances. Repeat to make four inner border strips total.

[5] Sew inner border strips to opposite edges of quilt center, noting direction of assorted print triangles. Press seams toward quilt center.

[6] Join mottled cream 6¼" squares to ends of remaining inner border strips. Press seams toward squares. Add remaining inner border strips to remaining edges of quilt center,

again noting direction of assorted print triangles. Press seams toward quilt center.

add outer border

[1] Cut and piece mottled cream 4½×42" strips to make:
  ▸ 2—4½×76½" outer border strips
  ▸ 2—4½×68½" outer border strips

[1] Sew short outer border strips to opposite edges of quilt center. Add long outer border strips to remaining edges to complete quilt top. Press all seams toward outer border.

finish quilt

[1] Layer quilt top, batting, and backing; baste. (For details, see Complete the Quilt, *page 174.*)

QUILTING DIAGRAM

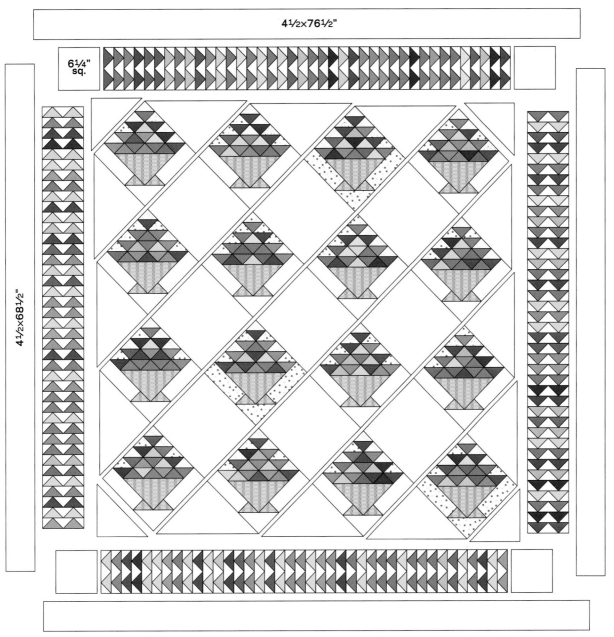

QUILT ASSEMBLY DIAGRAM

[2] Quilt as desired. The quilt shown was machine-quilted with feathered wreath designs in the mottled cream setting pieces and scallops in the blocks. Swirls were stitched in the inner border and a feather design was stitched in the outer border **(Quilting Diagram)**.

[3] Bind with blue plaid binding strips. (For details, see Complete the Quilt.)

sweet & simple

DESIGNER **BRENDA HAWKES**
PHOTOGRAPHER **ADAM ALBRIGHT**

materials

- ▸ 25—9×22" pieces (fat eighths) assorted prints in pink, lime green, and brown (blocks, border)
- ▸ 1¾ yards white tone-on-tone (blocks, setting and corner triangles)
- ▸ ⅝ yard brown-and-pink paisley (binding)
- ▸ 3 yards backing fabric
- ▸ 52" square batting

Finished quilt: 45½" square
Finished block: 7½" square

Quantities are for 44/45"-wide, 100% cotton fabrics. Measurements include ¼" seam allowances. Sew with right sides together unless otherwise stated.

cut fabrics

Cut pieces in the following order. Corner Cutting Pattern is on *Pattern Sheet 1*. To make and use templates for cutting the pattern, see Make and Use Templates on *page 170*.

From *each* assorted pink, lime green, and brown print, cut:
- ▸ 1—2×9" strip
- ▸ 2—3⅞" squares

From remaining assorted pink, lime green, and brown prints, cut:
- ▸ 116—2" squares

From white tone-on-tone, cut:
- ▸ 25—2×9" strips
- ▸ 3—11⅞" squares, cutting each diagonally twice in an X for 12 setting triangles total
- ▸ 2—6¼" squares, cutting each in half diagonally for 4 corner triangles total
- ▸ 50—3⅞" squares
- ▸ 25—2" squares

From brown-and-pink paisley, cut:
- ▸ Enough 2½"-wide bias strips to total 200" for binding (For details, see Cutting Bias Strips on *page 174*.)

assemble blocks

[1] For a Churn Dash block, gather a set of matching assorted print pieces (two 3⅞" squares and one 2×9" strip) and a set of white tone-on-tone pieces (two 3⅞" squares, one 2×9" strip, and one 2" square).

[2] Use a pencil to mark a diagonal line on wrong side of each white tone-on-tone 3⅞" square.

[3] Referring to **Diagram 1**, layer a marked white tone-on-tone square atop each print 3⅞" square. Sew each pair together with two seams, stitching ¼" on each side of drawn line. Cut each pair apart on drawn line to make two triangle units. Press each triangle unit open, pressing seam toward print fabric, to make four triangle-squares total.

[4] Join a white tone-on-tone 2×9" strip and a print 2×9" strip to make a strip set. Press seam toward print fabric. Cut strip set into four 2"-wide segments (Diagram 2).

DIAGRAM 1

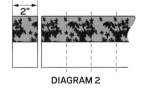

DIAGRAM 2

Easy piecing tricks make this Churn Dash quilt a fun weekend project.

[5] Referring to **Diagram 3**, lay out triangle-squares, 2"-wide segments, and white tone-on-tone 2" square in three rows. Sew together pieces in each row. Press seams toward 2"-wide segments. Join rows to make a Churn Dash block. Press seams in one direction. The block should be 8" square including seam allowances.

[6] Repeat steps 1–5 to make 25 Churn Dash blocks total.

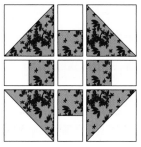

DIAGRAM 3

✺ COLOR OPTION ✺

Using dark and light background fabrics for the Churn Dash blocks adds extra interest to this version of Sweet & Simple. By planning the arrangement of the light blue block backgrounds, an eye-catching secondary pattern is formed within the quilt center.

assemble quilt center

[1] Referring to **Quilt Assembly Diagram,** lay out blocks and white tone-on-tone setting triangles in diagonal rows.

[2] Sew together pieces in each row. Press seams in one direction, alternating direction with each row. Join rows. Press seams in one direction.

[3] Add white tone-on-tone corner triangles to make quilt center. Press seams toward corner triangles. Trim quilt center to 42½" square including seam allowances.

assemble and add border

[1] Sew together 28 assorted print 2" squares to make a short border strip. Press seams in one direction. The short border strip should be 2×42½" including seam allowances. Repeat to make a second short border strip.

[2] Sew together 30 assorted print 2" squares to make a long border strip. Press seams in one direction. The long border strip should be 2×45½" including seam allowances. Repeat to make a second long border strip.

[3] Sew short border strips to opposite edges of quilt center. Add long border strips to remaining edges to complete quilt top. Press all seams toward quilt center.

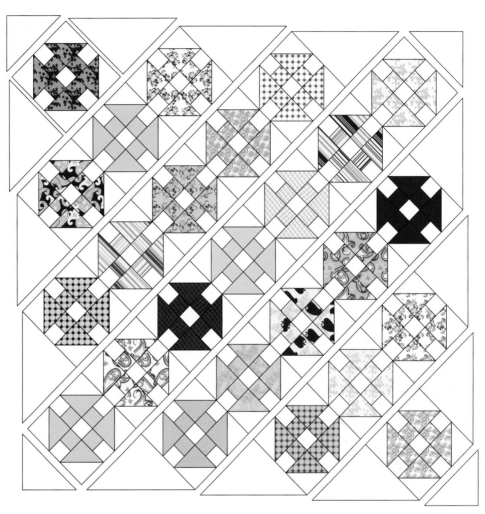

QUILT ASSEMBLY DIAGRAM

finish quilt

[1] Layer quilt top, batting, and backing; baste. (For details, see Complete the Quilt, *page 174.*)

[2] Quilt as desired. The featured quilt is machine-quilted with an allover meandering design.

[3] Using Corner Cutting Pattern, trace a curve at one corner of quilt top. Trim excess fabric and batting along marked curve **(Diagram 4).** Repeat to trim remaining corners.

[4] Bind with brown-and-pink paisley bias binding strips. (For details, see Complete the Quilt.)

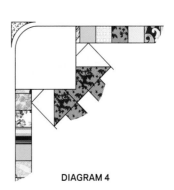

DIAGRAM 4

DESIGNER **PAM BUDA**
MACHINE QUILTER **RONDA DRANTER**
PHOTOGRAPHER **CAMERON SADEGHPOUR**

mix
it up

Mix and match 1930s prints in classic Jacob's Ladder blocks, then turn them about to create secondary 16-Patch designs.

materials
- 3½ yards muslin (blocks, borders)
- 5½ yards total assorted 1930s prints in pink, orange, yellow, green, teal, blue, and purple (blocks, borders, binding)
- 7¼ yards backing fabric
- 87" square batting

Finished quilt: 80½" square
Finished block: 6" square

Quantities are for 44/45"-wide, 100% cotton fabrics. Measurements include ¼" seam allowances. Sew with right sides together unless otherwise stated.

cut fabrics
Cut pieces in the following order.

From muslin, cut:
- 15—3¾×42" strips for inner and outer borders
- 100—3⅞" squares
- 80—2⅝" squares, cutting each in half diagonally for 160 triangles total

From assorted 1930s prints, cut:
- 19—2½×20" strips for binding
- 100 sets of one 2×9" strip and one matching 3⅞" square
- 100—2×9" strips (These are in addition to those just cut.)
- 40—4" squares
- 160—1¾" squares

assemble blocks

[1] Use a pencil to mark a diagonal line on wrong side of each muslin 3⅞" square.

[2] For one Jacob's Ladder block, gather a marked muslin square, a 2×9" strip, and a 3⅞" square from one 1930s print, and a 2×9" strip from a second 1930s print.

[3] Layer marked muslin square atop 1930s print 3⅞" square. Sew together with two seams, stitching ¼" on each side of drawn line (Diagram 1).

[4] Cut pair apart on drawn line to make two triangle units (Diagram 1). Open triangle units and press seams toward 1930s print to make two triangle-squares. Each triangle-square should be 3½" square including seam allowances.

[5] Sew together 1930s print 2×9" strips to make a strip set (Diagram 2). Press seam toward darker print. Cut strip set into four 2"-wide segments.

[6] Join two 2"-wide segments to make a large Four-Patch unit (Diagram 3). Press seam open. The unit should be 3½" square including seam allowances. Repeat to make a second large Four-Patch unit.

[7] Referring to Diagram 4, lay out triangle-squares and large Four-Patch units in pairs. Sew together pieces in each pair; press seams open. Join pairs to make a Jacob's Ladder block; press seam open. The block should be 6½" square including seam allowances.

[8] Repeat steps 2–7 to make 100 Jacob's Ladder blocks total.

assemble quilt center

[1] Referring to Quilt Assembly Diagram on *page 56*, lay out blocks in 10 rows, rotating every other block a quarter turn. Sew together blocks in each row. Press seams in one direction, alternating direction with each row.

[2] Join rows to make quilt center. Press seams in one direction. The quilt center should be 60½" square including seam allowances.

assemble and add borders

[1] Cut and piece muslin 3¾×42" strips to make:
   ▸ 2—3¾×80½" outer border strips
   ▸ 2—3¾×74" outer border strips
   ▸ 2—3¾×67" inner border strips
   ▸ 2—3¾×60½" inner border strips

[2] Sew short inner border strips to opposite edges of quilt center. Add long inner border strips to remaining edges. Press all seams toward inner border.

[3] Join four assorted 1930s print 1¾" squares in pairs (Diagram 5). Press seams in opposite directions. Join pairs to make a small Four-Patch unit. Press seam in one direction. The small Four-Patch unit should be 3" square including seam allowances. Repeat to make 40 small Four-Patch units total.

[4] Sew muslin triangles to opposite edges of a small Four-Patch unit (Diagram 6). Add muslin triangles to remaining edges to make a Square-in-a-Square unit. Press all seams toward triangles. The unit should be 4" square including seam allowances. Repeat to make 40 Square-in-a-Square units total.

DIAGRAM 1

DIAGRAM 2

DIAGRAM 3

DIAGRAM 4

DIAGRAM 5

DIAGRAM 6

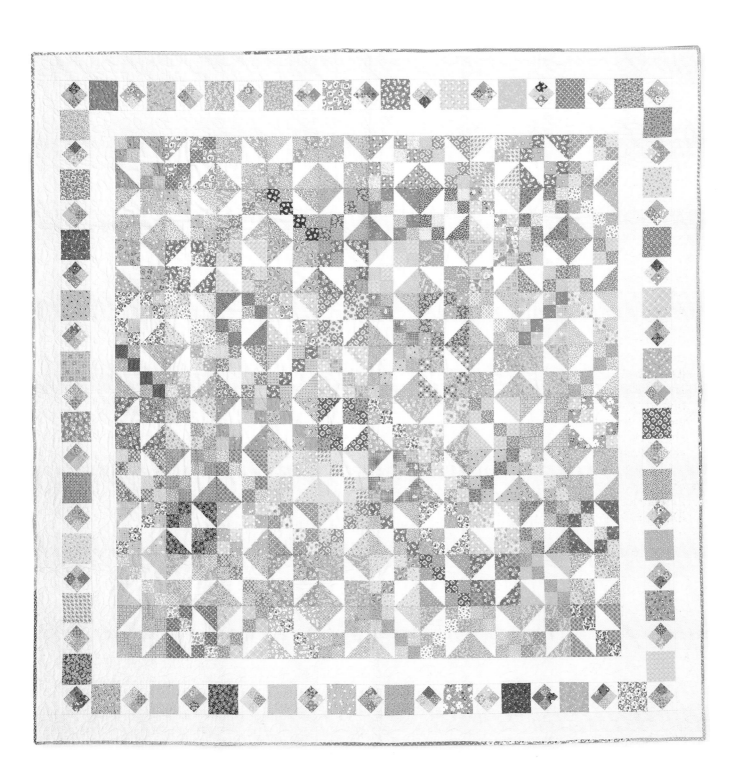

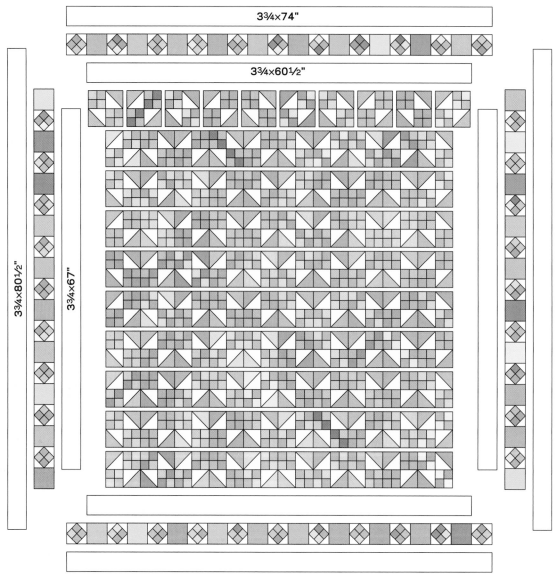

QUILT ASSEMBLY DIAGRAM

[5] Referring to **Quilt Assembly Diagram,** join 10 assorted 1930s print 4" squares and nine Square-in-a-Square units in a row to make a short middle border strip. Press seams toward squares. The short middle border strip should be 4×67" including seam allowances.

Repeat to make a second short middle border strip. Sew short middle border strips to opposite edges of quilt center.

[6] Join 10 assorted 1930s print 4" squares and 11 Square-in-a-Square units in a row to make a long middle border strip. Press

seams toward squares. The long middle border strip should be 4×74" including seam allowances. Repeat to make a second long middle border strip. Add long middle border strips to remaining edges of quilt center. Press all seams toward inner border.

[7] Sew short outer border strips to opposite edges of quilt center. Add long outer border strips to remaining edges to complete quilt top. Press all seams toward outer border.

finish quilt

[1] Layer quilt top, batting, and backing; baste. (For details, see Complete the Quilt, *page 174*.)

[2] Quilt as desired. This quilt was machine-quilted with a flower motif in each large Four-Patch unit and a loop design in the 1930s print triangles at block intersections (Quilting Diagram). A flower-and-leaf vine was quilted in the muslin borders and two medallion motifs were quilted in the middle border.

[3] Using diagonal seams, join assorted 1930s print 2½×20" strips to make a pieced binding strip. Bind with pieced binding strip. (For details, see Complete the Quilt.)

QUILTING DIAGRAM

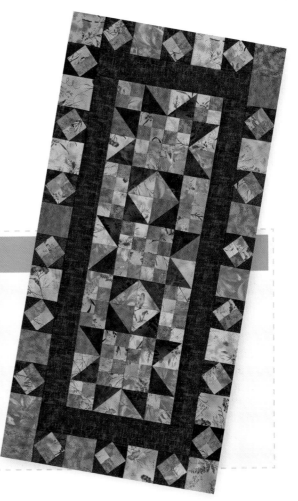

☼ COLOR OPTION ☼

For this version of Mix It Up, a monochromatic palette of browns mix with cool blue to make a table runner with a serene feeling.

To make the pieced outer border fit the three-block quilt center, cut the short inner border strips 3½" wide and the long inner border strips 3¼" wide.

scrap happy

DESIGNER **MONICA SOLORIO-SNOW** QUILTMAKER **JUDY SOHN**
QUILTER **LEANNE OLSON** PHOTOGRAPHER **SCOTT LITTLE**

Sash squares of reproduction fabrics with polka dot strips and colorful stripe squares to make each pretty print stand out.

materials

- 58—5" squares assorted red, blue, green, and yellow prints (blocks)
- 1 yard white-and-blue polka dot (sashing, inner border)
- ⅓ yard solid red (middle border)
- ⅛ yard *total* assorted red, green, and blue stripe (sashing squares)
- ¾ yard blue floral (outer border)
- ½ yard blue dot (binding)
- 2⅞ yards backing fabric
- 49×63" batting

Finished quilt: 42¾×57"

Quantities are for 44/45"-wide, 100% cotton fabrics. Measurements include a ¼" seam allowance. Sew with right sides together unless otherwise stated.

cut fabrics

To make the best use of your fabrics, cut pieces in the following order.

From assorted red, blue, green, and yellow prints, cut:
- 58—4½" squares

From white-and-blue polka dot, cut:
- 5—2½×42" strips for inner border
- 96—1½×4½" rectangles

From solid red, cut:
- 5—1½×42" strips for middle border

From *each* assorted red, green, and blue stripe, cut:
- 20—1½" squares

From blue floral, cut:
- 5—4½×42" strips for outer border

From blue dot, cut:
- 6—2½×42" binding strips

assemble quilt center

[1] Referring to photograph *opposite* and **Quilt Center Assembly Diagram,** lay out the 58 assorted red, blue, green, and yellow print 4½" squares; 96 white-and-blue polka dot sashing rectangles; and 59 red, green, and blue stripe 1½" squares in diagonal rows.

[2] Sew together pieces in each row. Press seams toward sashing strips. Join rows to make quilt center. Press seams toward sashing rows.

[3] Referring to **Cutting Diagram,** trim quilt center ¼" beyond midpoints of sashing squares along each edge. Monica recommends stay-stitching ⅛" from edge of quilt center to prevent the bias outer edges from stretching. The quilt center should be 28¾×43" including seam allowances.

QUILT CENTER ASSEMBLY DIAGRAM

CUTTING DIAGRAM

assemble and add borders

[1] Cut and piece white-and-blue polka dot 2½×42"strips to make:
  ‣ 2—2½×43" inner border strips
  ‣ 2—2½×32¾" inner border strips

[2] Sew long inner border strips to long edges of quilt center. Add short inner border strips to remaining edges. Press all seams toward inner border.

[3] Cut and piece solid red 1½×42" strips to make:
  ‣ 2—1½×47" middle border strips
  ‣ 2—1½×34¾" middle border strips

[4] Join long middle border strips to long edges of quilt center. Add short middle border strips to remaining edges. Press all seams toward middle border.

[5] Cut and piece blue floral 4½×42" strips to make:
  ‣ 2—4½×49" outer border strips
  ‣ 2—4½×42¾" outer border strips

[6] Sew long outer border strips to long edges of quilt center. Add short outer border strips to remaining edges. Press all seams toward outer border.

finish quilt

[1] Layer quilt top, batting, and backing; baste. (For details, see Complete the Quilt, *page 174*.)

[2] Quilt as desired.

[3] Bind with blue dot binding strips. (For details, see Complete the Quilt.)

»TIP«

If you need to press a dark seam allowance toward a light piece, trim the sewn darker seam allowance slightly to prevent it from showing through .

QUILT ASSEMBLY DIAGRAM

rich & warm

cinnamon & nutmeg

DESIGNER **TARA LYNN DARR** QUILTER **DEBBIE CRAMER** PHOTOGRAPHER **CAMERON SADEGHPOUR**

Spicy red and warm brown reproduction fabrics cut in angular shapes offer a distinctive look. Strip piecing and rotary cutting make quick work of the double bed–size quilt.

materials

- 13—¼-yard pieces assorted red prints (blocks)
- 10—¼-yard pieces assorted brown prints (blocks)
- 9—¼-yard pieces assorted tan and cream prints (blocks)
- 4 yards dark tan print (sashing, outer border)
- 2⅛ yards dark brown print (sashing, inner border, binding)
- 8 yards backing fabric
- 96×109" batting

Finished quilt: 89¾×102½"

Quantities are for 44/45"-wide, 100% cotton fabrics. Measurements include ¼" seam allowances. Sew with right sides together unless otherwise stated.

cut fabrics

Cut pieces in the following order.

We recommend rotary-cutting all of the pieces—including the diamonds and triangles—needed for this quilt. Instructions that follow are for this method.

A 6½×24" acrylic ruler marked with 30° and 60° angles is most helpful when cutting pieces for this project. That size ruler is shown in the diagrams. (Instructions are given for right-handed cutting; if you're left-handed, reverse diagrams and directions.)

If you'd rather use templates to construct the quilt (or wish to double-check that the shapes you're rotary cutting are accurate), patterns are on *Pattern Sheet 1*. For details on using templates, see Make and Use Templates, *page 170*.

From assorted red, brown, tan, and cream prints, cut:
- 18—6½×42" strips
- 36—2½×42" strips

From dark tan print, cut:
- 54—2½×42" strips (44 for sashing and 10 for outer border)

From dark brown print, cut:
- 22—2½×42" strips (10 for binding and 12 for sashing)
- 10—1½×42" strips for inner border

prepare large pieces

[1] Referring to **Diagram 1**, trim right-hand edge of a red, brown, tan, or cream print 6½×42" strip at a 60° angle. To do this, align 60° line of an acrylic ruler (blue line on diagram) with top edge of strip; cut along right-hand edge of ruler.

[2] Rotate strip 180°. Measure 6½" from trimmed (left-hand) edge and, cutting parallel to trimmed edge, cut to make a large diamond (**Diagram 2**). Repeat to cut three large diamonds total.

[3] Repeat steps 1 and 2 with remaining red, brown, tan, and cream print 6½×42" strips, cutting two or three diamonds from each strip to make 40 large diamonds total. (Retain remaining partial strips to use in the next two steps.)

[4] Select a Step 3 red, brown, tan, or cream print partial strip. The left-hand edge already should be cut at a 60° angle. (If it's not, repeat Step 1 to trim.) Referring to **Diagram 3**, measure ½" from corner along bottom edge of strip and make a mark. Align ruler with mark and cut at a 30° angle to make a large half diamond. Repeat to make 10 large half diamonds total.

[5] Select a Step 3 red, brown, tan, or cream print partial strip. The left-hand edge already should be cut at a 60° angle. (If it's not, repeat Step 1 to trim.) Referring to **Diagram 4**,

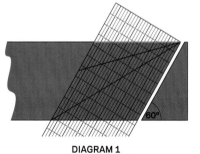

DIAGRAM 1

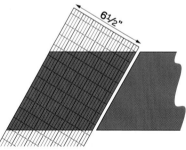

6½"

DIAGRAM 2

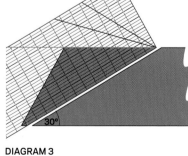

30°

½"

DIAGRAM 3

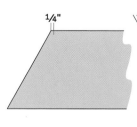

¼"

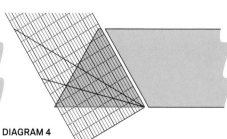

DIAGRAM 4

measure ¼" from corner along top edge of strip and make a mark. Align ruler with mark and cut at a 60° angle to make a large triangle. Repeat to make 20 large triangles total.

[6] On a large triangle, measure ¼" from top right-hand corner of "flattened" tip and make a mark (Diagram 5). Holding ruler vertically, align its edge with mark; trim along ruler edge to make a corner triangle A. Repeat with a second triangle to make a second corner triangle A.

[7] Measuring from top left-hand corners of two large triangles' flattened tips, repeat Step 6 to make two corner B triangles total (Diagram 6).

prepare sashing pieces

[1] Referring to Diagram 7 and Prepare Large Pieces, *page 66*, steps 1 and 2, trim one end of a dark brown print 2½×42" strip at a 60° angle and cut it into ten 2½"-wide sashing diamonds. Repeat with nine of the remaining dark brown print 2½×42" strips to cut 93 sashing diamonds total. (Retain remaining partial strips for use in Step 3.)

[2] Trim one end of a remaining dark brown print 2½×42" strip at a 60° angle. Referring to Diagram 8 and Prepare Large Pieces, Step 5, cut strip into 10 sashing triangles. Repeat with a second dark brown print 2½×42" strip to cut

>> TIP <<

Check every two or three rows to ensure you're still cutting at a perfect 60° angle; retrim to correct the angle, if needed.

18 sashing triangles total. (Retain remaining partial strips for use in Step 3.)

[3] Referring to Diagram 9 and Prepare Large Pieces, Step 4, use a dark brown print partial strip to cut a sashing half diamond. Repeat to cut 12 sashing half diamonds total.

[4] Trim one end of a dark tan print 2½×42" strip at a 60° angle. Positioning ruler parallel with angled end of strip, trim 6½" from angled end to make a sashing strip A (Diagram 10). Repeat to cut 108 A sashing strips total.

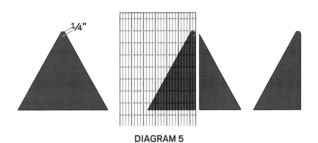

DIAGRAM 5

DIAGRAM 6

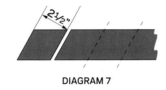

DIAGRAM 7

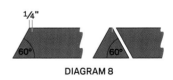

DIAGRAM 8

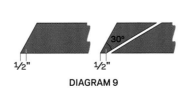

DIAGRAM 9

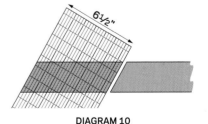

DIAGRAM 10

[5] Flip ruler over and repeat Step 4 with the 60° angles running in opposite direction to cut a B sashing strip (Diagram 11). Repeat to cut 108 B sashing strips total.

assemble pieced diamonds

[1] Sew together three assorted red, brown, tan, or cream print 2½×42" strips to make a strip set (Diagram 12). Press seams in one direction. Repeat to make 12 strip sets total.

[2] Referring to Prepare Large Pieces, Step 1, cut left-hand edge of a strip set at a 60° angle. Measure 6½" from trimmed edge and cut to make a pieced A diamond (Diagram 13). Repeat to make 27 pieced A diamonds total.

[3] Flip ruler over and repeat Step 2 with the 60° angles running in opposite direction to cut a pieced B diamond (Diagram 14). Repeat to make 27 pieced B diamonds total.

assemble quilt center

[1] Referring to Quilt Assembly Diagram, lay out all prepared pieces, except for corner triangles, in diagonal rows. Pay attention to placement of A and B diamonds and sashing strips. Position large and small triangles with their flattened tips (the ¼"-long edge) running parallel to top and bottom edges of quilt center. This will help you match up pieces and ensure grain line runs in correct direction in finished quilt.

[2] To assemble a row, layer first triangle and its adjacent sashing strip with raw edges aligned; sew together (Diagram 15). Press seam toward sashing strip.

[3] To add a pieced diamond, layer it with the sashing strip so the raw edges are aligned but the ends are offset; sides of pieces should meet exactly at ¼" seam line (Diagram 16). Join pieces and press seam toward sashing strip. Add remaining pieces in same manner to complete row, pressing all seams toward sashing strips. Repeat to sew together pieces in each diagonal row.

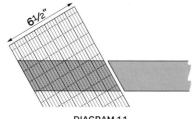

DIAGRAM 11

DIAGRAM 12

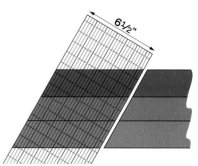

DIAGRAM 13

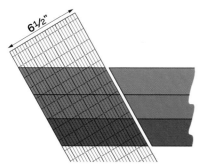

DIAGRAM 14

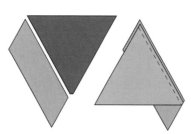

DIAGRAM 15

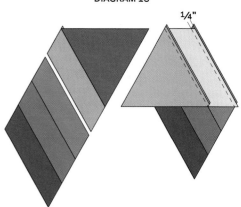

DIAGRAM 16

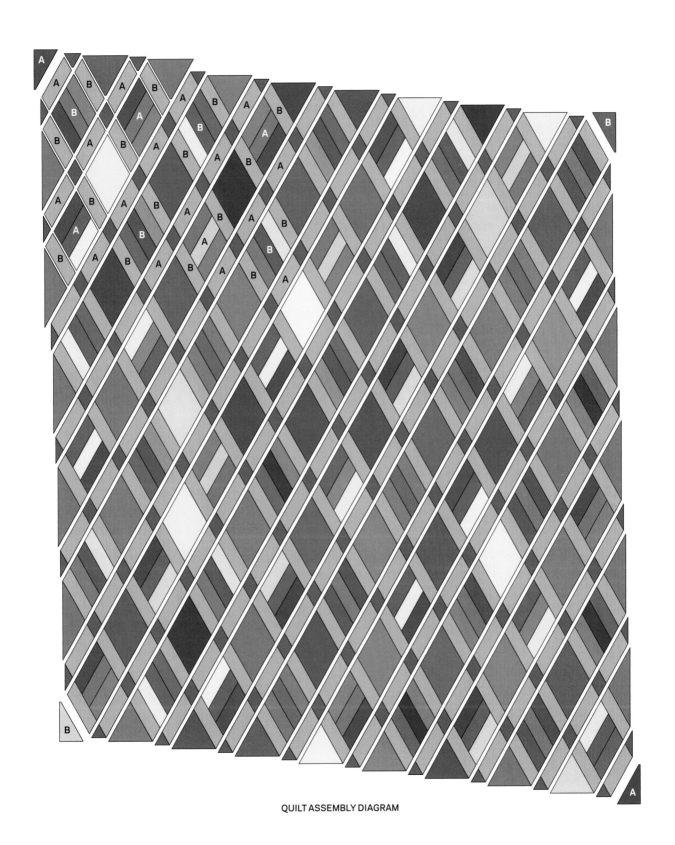

QUILT ASSEMBLY DIAGRAM

[4] Join rows and add corner triangles to make quilt center. Press seams in one direction. The quilt center should be 83¾×96½" including seam allowances.

assemble and add borders

[1] Cut and piece dark brown print 1½×42" strips to make:
- 2—1½×96½" inner border strips
- 2—1½×85¾" inner border strips

[2] Sew long inner border strips to long edges of quilt center. Add short inner border strips to remaining edges. Press all seams toward inner border.

[3] Cut and piece dark tan print 2½×42" strips to make:
- 2—2½×98½" outer border strips
- 2—2½×89¾" outer border strips

[4] Sew long outer border strips to long edges of quilt center. Sew short outer border strips to remaining edges to complete quilt top. Press all seams toward outer border.

finish quilt

[1] Layer quilt top, batting, and backing; baste. (For details, see Complete the Quilt, *page 174*.)

[2] Quilt as desired. This quilt was machine-quilted with an allover leaf design (Quilting Diagram).

[3] Bind with dark brown print binding strips. (For details, see Complete the Quilt.)

QUILTING DIAGRAM

☼ COLOR OPTION ☼

Do you want to make a quilt as a baby shower gift but have only a few days to get it done? In this version of Cinnamon & Nutmeg, the large diamonds are single pieces of fabric, rather than the pieced strips of the original.

DESIGNER **FLAVIN GLOVER**
PHOTOGRAPHER **ADAM ALBRIGHT**

log cabin STARS

Intricate color play, carefully pieced units, and a striking setting play up the versatility of the much-loved Log Cabin block.

materials

- 9×22" piece (fat eighth) green print (block centers)
- 1½ yards total assorted purple prints and solids (blocks A, B, and E)
- 1⅛ yard total assorted yellow-orange prints (blocks A, C, D, and E)
- 5—18×22" pieces (fat quarters) assorted light green and gold prints (Block B)
- 5—9×22" pieces (fat eighths) assorted multicolor prints (Block C)
- 5—9×22" pieces (fat eighths) assorted dark purple prints (Block D)
- ¾ yard dark green floral (blocks F, G, H, I)
- 18×22" piece (fat quarter) each of solid black and black print (blocks F, G, H, I)
- ¾ yard mottled olive green (inner and outer borders)
- ⅓ yard mottled light green (middle border)
- ¾ yard purple stripe (binding)
- 3⅔ yards backing fabric
- 66" square batting

Finished quilt: 59¼" square
Finished blocks: 5¼" square

Quantities are for 44/45"-wide, 100% cotton fabrics. Measurements include ¼" seam allowances. Sew with right sides together unless otherwise stated.

>> TIP <<

"Cut strips for Log Cabin blocks parallel to the selvages, which are on the fabric's lengthwise grain. Strips cut lengthwise are consistently straighter and have less stretch than those cut on the crosswise grain. I make an exception for stripes and defined patterns that appear more distinctive when cut crosswise."

—DESIGNER FLAVIN GLOVER

cut fabrics

Cut pieces in the following order. For easy piecing, sort pieces into separate bags according to position number 1–7.

From green print, cut:
- 60—1¼" squares for position 1

From assorted purple prints and solids, cut:
- 56—1¼×5¾" rectangles for position 7
- 144—1¼×4¼" rectangles for positions 5 and 6
- 144—1¼×2¾" rectangles for positions 3 and 4
- 56—1¼" squares for positions 1 and 2

From assorted yellow-orange prints, cut:
- 56—1¼×5¾" rectangles for position 7
- 80—1¼×4¼" rectangles for positions 5 and 6
- 80—1¼×2¾" rectangles for positions 3 and 4
- 72—1¼" squares for position 2

From each of the 5 light green or gold prints, cut:
- 4—1¼×5¾" rectangles for position 7
- 8—1¼×4¼" rectangles for positions 5 and 6
- 8—1¼×2¾" rectangles for positions 3 and 4
- 4—1¼" squares for position 2

From each of the 5 multicolor prints, cut:
- 2—1¼×5¾" rectangles for position 7
- 4—1¼×4¼" rectangles for positions 5 and 6
- 4—1¼×2¾" rectangles for positions 3 and 4
- 2—1¼" squares for position 2

From each of the 5 dark purple prints, cut:
- 2—1¼×5¾" rectangles for position 7
- 4—1¼×4¼" rectangles for positions 5 and 6
- 4—1¼×2¾" rectangles for positions 3 and 4
- 2—1¼" squares for position 2

From dark green floral, cut:
- 16—1¼×5¾" rectangles for position 7
- 60—1¼×4¼" rectangles for positions 5 and 6
- 88—1¼×2¾" rectangles for positions 3 and 4
- 22—1¼" squares for position 1

From solid black, cut:
- 8—1¼×5¾" rectangles for position 7
- 8—1¼×4¼" rectangles for position 6
- 44—1¼" squares for position 2

From black print, cut:
- 20—1¼×5¾" rectangles for position 7
- 20—1¼×4¼" rectangles for position 6

From mottled olive green, cut:
- 12—2×42" strips for inner and outer borders

From mottled light green, cut:
- 6—1½×42" strips for middle border

From purple stripe, cut:
- Enough 2½"-wide bias strips to total 260" in length for binding (For details, see Cutting Bias Strips, *page 174.*)

assemble block A

[1] For Block A, gather one each of the following pieces: green print position 1 square for block center; assorted purple print position 2 square and positions 3, 4, 5, 6, and 7 rectangles; and assorted yellow-orange print position 2 square and positions 3, 4, 5, 6, and 7 rectangles.

[2] Referring to **Diagram 1**, sew purple print and yellow-orange print position 2 squares to opposite edges of green print position 1 block center; press seams away from block center.

[3] Add purple print and yellow-orange print position 3 rectangles to long edges of Step 2 unit **(Diagram 2)**. Press seams away from block center.

[4] Referring to **Diagram 3**, continue adding rectangles in numerical order to make Log Cabin Block A. Press all seams away from block center. The block should be 5¾" square including seam allowances.

[5] Repeat steps 1–4 to make 20 total of Log Cabin Block A.

DIAGRAM 1 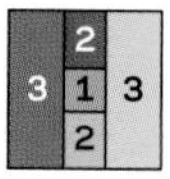   **DIAGRAM 2**

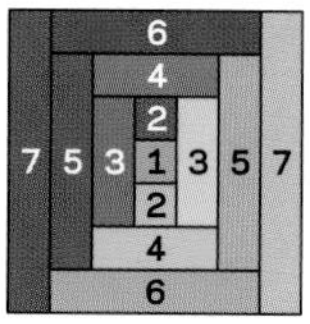

**BLOCK A
DIAGRAM 3**

assemble block B

[1] For Block B, gather one each of the following pieces: green print position 1 square for block center; assorted purple print position 2 square and positions 3, 4, 5, 6, and 7 rectangles; and matching light green or gold print position 2 square and positions 3, 4, 5, 6, and 7 rectangles.

[2] Using pieces from Step 1, refer to **Diagram 4** and Assemble Block A, steps 2-4, to make a Log Cabin Block B.

[3] Repeat steps 1 and 2 to make 20 total of Log Cabin Block B.

assemble block C

[1] For Block C, gather one each of the following pieces: green print position 1 square for block center; matching multicolor print position 2 square and positions 3, 4, 5, 6, and 7 rectangles; and assorted yellow-orange position 2 square and positions 3, 4, 5, 6, and 7 rectangles.

[2] Using pieces from Step 1, refer to **Diagram 5** and Assemble Block A, steps 2-4, to make a Log Cabin Block C.

[3] Repeat steps 1 and 2 to make 10 total of Log Cabin Block C.

assemble block D

[1] For Block D, gather one each of the following pieces: green print position 1 square for block center; matching dark purple print position 2 square and positions 3, 4, 5, 6, and 7 rectangles; and assorted yellow-orange position 2 square and positions 3, 4, 5, 6, and 7 rectangles.

[2] Using pieces from Step 1, refer to **Diagram 6** and Assemble Block A, steps 2-4, to make a Log Cabin Block D.

[3] Repeat steps 1 and 2 to make 10 total of Log Cabin Block D.

assemble block E

[1] For Block E, gather pieces from assorted purple prints (one position 1 square for block center; two each of positions 3, 4, 5, and 6 rectangles; and one position 7 rectangle) and assorted yellow-orange prints (two position 2 squares and one position 7 rectangle).

[2] Using pieces from Step 1, refer to **Diagram 7** and Assemble Block A, steps 2-4, to make a Log Cabin Block E.

[3] Repeat steps 1 and 2 to make 16 total of Log Cabin Block E.

>> TIP <<

Whether you construct this quilt with leftover strips from a multitude of fabrics or select just a few, look for great variation in scale so the logs in each block appear distinctive even though they're close in color.

assemble remaining blocks and setting triangles

[1] For Block F, gather one dark green floral position 1 square for block center and two each of these pieces: solid black position 2 squares, solid black positions 6 and 7 rectangles, and dark green floral positions 3, 4, and 5 rectangles.

[2] Using pieces from Step 1, refer to **Diagram 8** and Assemble Block A, steps 2-4, to make a Log Cabin Block F.

[3] Repeat steps 1 and 2 to make four total of Log Cabin Block F.

**BLOCK B
DIAGRAM 4**

**BLOCK C
DIAGRAM 5**

**BLOCK D
DIAGRAM 6**

**BLOCK E
DIAGRAM 7**

**BLOCK F
DIAGRAM 8**

**F SETTING TRIANGLES
DIAGRAM 9**

❋ COLOR OPTION ❋

Vivid red star points jump off the quilt while more muted gold star points recede, forming Friendship Stars that appear to float on top of one another in this vivid version of Log Cabin Stars. The middle border was fussy-cut with a print featuring the ABCs.

[4] Referring to **Diagram 9**, cut a Log Cabin Block F in half diagonally to make two F Setting Triangles. Repeat to make eight F Setting Triangles total.

[5] Using black print instead of solid black for the positions 6 and 7 rectangles, repeat steps 1–3 to make four of Log Cabin Block G. Cut them into eight G Setting Triangles **(Diagram 10).**

[6] For Block H, gather pieces from dark green floral (one position 1 square for block center; two each of positions 3, 4, and 5 rectangles; and one each of positions 6 and 7 rectangles), solid black (two position 2 squares), and black print (one each of position 6 and 7 rectangles).

[7] Using pieces from Step 6, refer to **Diagram 11** and Assemble Block A, steps 2–4, to make a Log Cabin Block H.

[8] Repeat steps 6 and 7 to make 12 total of Log Cabin Block H. Cut four of these blocks in half diagonally to make eight H Setting Triangles **(Diagram 11).**

[9] For Block I, gather pieces from dark green floral (one position 1 square for block center and two each of positions 3, 4, 5, 6 and 7 rectangles) and solid black (two position 2 squares).

[10] Using pieces from Step 9, refer to Diagram 12 and Assemble Block A, steps 2–4, to make a Log Cabin Block I.

[11] Repeat steps 9 and 10 to make a second Log Cabin Block I. Cut both in half diagonally to make four I Setting Triangles **(Diagram 12).**

BLOCK G

G SETTING TRIANGLES

DIAGRAM 10

BLOCK H

H SETTING TRIANGLES

DIAGRAM 11

BLOCK I

I SETTING TRIANGLES

DIAGRAM 12

assemble quilt center

[1] Referring to **Quilt Assembly Diagram** for placement, lay out all blocks and setting triangles in diagonal rows, rotating blocks as shown.

[2] Sew together pieces in each diagonal row. (Where each setting triangle joins a Log Cabin block, match up a straight edge of the setting triangle with the block; in this quilt, the point of the setting triangle does not extend beyond the edge of the block.) Press seams in one direction, alternating direction with each row.

[3] Join rows to complete quilt center. Press all seams toward bottom right-hand corner. Trim points of Log Cabin blocks that extend beyond edges of setting triangles. The quilt center should be 51¼" square including seam allowances.

add borders

[1] Cut and piece mottled olive green 2×42" strips to make:
  ‣ 2—2×59¼" outer border strips
  ‣ 2—2×56¼" outer border strips
  ‣ 2—2×54¼" inner border strips
  ‣ 2—2×51¼" inner border strips

[2] Sew short inner border strips to opposite edges of quilt center. Add long inner border strips to remaining edges. Press all seams toward inner border.

[3] Cut and piece mottled light green 1½×42" strips to make:
  ‣ 2—1½×56¼" middle border strips
  ‣ 2—1½×54¼" middle border strips

[4] Sew short middle border strips to opposite edges of quilt center. Add long middle border strips to remaining edges. Press all seams toward middle border.

[5] Sew short outer border strips to opposite edges of quilt center. Add long outer border strips to remaining edges to complete quilt top. Press all seams toward outer border.

finish quilt

[1] Layer quilt top, batting, and backing; baste. (For details, see Complete the Quilt, *page 174*.)

[2] Quilt as desired. In each star, designer Flavin Glover hand-quilted a three-quarter daisy motif in the star points and a starburst in the center (**Quilting Diagram**). She stitched in the ditch in the remaining Log Cabin blocks and added an orange peel design in the borders.

[3] Bind with purple stripe bias binding strips. (For details, see Complete the Quilt.)

QUILTING DIAGRAM

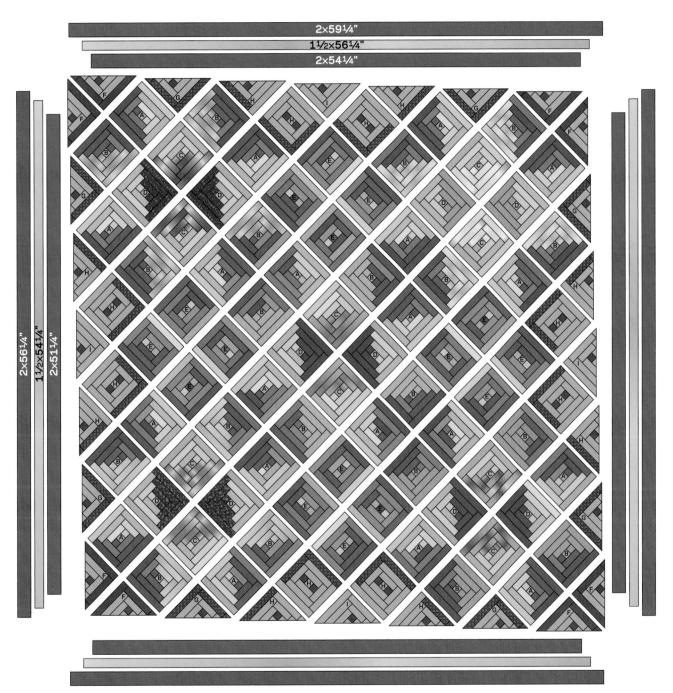

QUILT ASSEMBLY DIAGRAM

DESIGNER **CARRIE NELSON**
QUILTER **DIANE TRICKA**
PHOTOGRAPHER **CAMERON SADEGHPOUR**

pick & mix

Fabric bits and pieces are everywhere in this quilt, including the sashing, borders, and binding. You'll love digging into your stash to come up with just the right mixture. The sashing may look complicated but actually is simple—just combine fabric strips, then trim to fit.

materials

- 3⅔ yards total or 15—18×22" pieces (fat quarters) assorted light prints (blocks, border)
- 6¼ yards total or 30—18×22" pieces (fat quarters) assorted medium and dark prints (blocks, sashing, border, binding)
- 7⅛ yards backing fabric
- 85" square batting

Finished quilt: 78½" square
Finished block: 12" square

Quantities are for 44/45"-wide, 100% cotton fabrics. Measurements include ¼" seam allowances. Sew with right sides together unless otherwise stated.

cut fabrics

Cut pieces in the following order.

From assorted light prints, cut:
- 100 sets of one 2×9" strip and one matching 3⅞" square
- 48—3⅞" squares (These are in addition to those just cut.)
- 4—3½" squares

From assorted medium and dark prints, cut:
- 28—2½×14" binding strips
- 100—2×9" strips
- 286—1½×6½" strips
- 148—3⅞" squares

assemble triangle-squares

[1] Use a pencil to mark a diagonal line on wrong side of each light print 3⅞" square.

[2] Layer each marked light print square atop a medium or dark print 3⅞" square. Sew each pair together with two seams, stitching ¼" on each side of drawn line (Diagram 1).

[3] Cut a pair apart on drawn line to make two triangle units (Diagram 1). Open triangle units and press seams toward dark prints to make two triangle-squares. Each triangle-square should be 3½" square including seam allowances.

[4] Repeat Step 3 with remaining pairs to make 296 triangle-squares total (148 sets of two matching triangle-squares).

assemble four-patch units

[1] Sew together a light print 2×9" strip and a medium or dark print 2×9" strip to make a strip set (Diagram 2). Press seam toward darker print. Cut strip set into four 2"-wide segments.

DIAGRAM 1   DIAGRAM 2

[2] Join two 2"-wide segments to make a Four-Patch unit (Diagram 3). To reduce bulk where multiple seams meet, designer Carrie Nelson suggests removing a few stitches at the seam intersection. Fan out seam allowances and press them flat, forming a tiny Four-Patch on the fabric wrong side (Pressing Diagram). Press seams in all units in same direction (clockwise in diagram shown) so seams will abut when units are joined together. The unit should be 3½" square including seam allowances. Repeat to make a second Four-Patch unit.

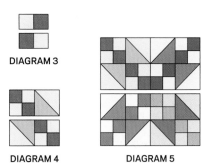

DIAGRAM 3

DIAGRAM 4   DIAGRAM 5

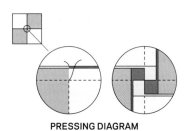

PRESSING DIAGRAM

[3] Repeat steps 1 and 2 to make 200 Four-Patch units total (100 sets of two matching units).

assemble blocks

[1] For one Buckeye Beauty unit, gather two matching triangle-squares and two matching Four-Patch units, all with the same light print.

[2] Referring to Diagram 4, lay out triangle-squares and Four-Patch units in pairs. Sew together pieces in each pair; press seams toward Four-Patch units. Join pairs to make a Buckeye Beauty unit; press seams clockwise as in Assemble Four-Patch Units, Step 2. The Buckeye Beauty unit should be 6½" square including seam allowances.

[3] Repeat steps 1 and 2 to make 100 Buckeye Beauty units total.

[4] Referring to Diagram 5, lay out four Buckeye Beauty units in pairs, rotating units as shown. Join units in each pair. Press seams in opposite directions.

[5] Join pairs to make a block; press seams clockwise as in Step 2. The block should be 12½" square including seam allowances.

[6] Repeat steps 4 and 5 to make 25 blocks total.

make sashing strips and rectangles

[1] Sew together 13 assorted medium and dark print 1½×6½" rectangles along short edges to make a pieced strip (Diagram 6). Press seams in one direction. Repeat to make 22 pieced strips total.

[2] Aligning long edges, lay out two pieced strips, offsetting them by about 3" (Diagram 7). Join pieced strips to make a pieced strip pair; press seam open. Repeat to make 11 pieced strip pairs total.

[3] Trim a pieced strip pair to 2½×72½" to make a pieced sashing strip (Diagram 8). Repeat to make six pieced sashing strips total.

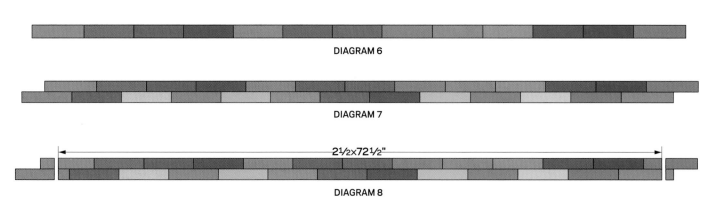

DIAGRAM 6

DIAGRAM 7

2½×72½"

DIAGRAM 8

pull it together

Particularly in scrappy quilts, designer Carrie Nelson prefers a pieced sashing and border to prevent any one fabric from dominating the overall design. "If I had used a blue fabric for the sashing in Pick & Mix, it would appear to be a blue quilt even if there weren't any blue prints in the blocks," Carrie says. "And if I had cut sashing rectangles from the various fat quarters, some sashing strips would be more dominant because of a stronger color, print, or value." Keeping it all scrappy maintains a balanced look across the finished quilt top. If you prefer a more planned approach, use the **Coloring Diagram** on *Pattern Sheet 2* to try out different color schemes.

[4] Cut each remaining pieced strip pair into six 2½×12½" segments (Diagram 9) to make 30 pieced sashing rectangles total.

assemble quilt center

[1] Referring to Quilt Assembly Diagram, lay out blocks, sashing strips, and sashing rectangles in rows. Sew together pieces in each block row. Press seams toward sashing rectangles.

[2] Join block rows and sashing strips to make quilt center. Press seams toward sashing.

The quilt center should be 72½" square including seam allowances.

assemble and add border

[1] Referring to Quilt Assembly Diagram, join 24 triangle-squares to make a border strip. Press seams in one direction. The strip should be 3½×72½" including seam allowances. Repeat to make four border strips total.

[2] Sew border strips to opposite edges of quilt center. Press seams toward sashing.

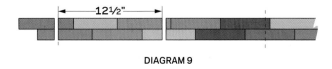

DIAGRAM 9

12½"

don't forget the back

If you have to piece a backing, take the opportunity to make the quilt back interesting. For Pick & Mix, designer Carrie Nelson pieced a 9½×45½" row from leftover Four-Patch units.

>> **TIP** <<

To prevent the pieced border seams from separating while you quilt and bind this project, machine-baste a scant ¼" from the outer edge around the entire quilt top. This will stabilize the border and keep your quilt in shape.

[3] Sew light print 3½" squares to each end of remaining border strips. Press seams toward light print squares. Add pieced border strips to remaining edges of quilt center to complete quilt top. Press seams toward sashing.

finish quilt

[1] Layer quilt top, batting, and backing; baste. (For details, see Complete the Quilt, *page 174*.)

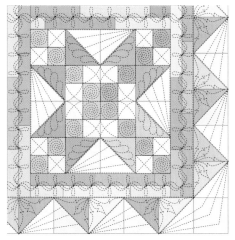

QUILTING DIAGRAM

QUILT ASSEMBLY DIAGRAM

[2] Quilt as desired. This quilt features machine-quilted blocks with a swirl in each medium and dark print square, an X in each light print square, a feather motif in each medium and dark print triangle, and radiating lines across the light print triangles **(Quilting Diagram)**. It was also stitched in the ditch around the block units, sashing, and border, then a continuous loop design was added in the sashing and a flame design was added in the medium and dark triangles of the border.

[3] Using diagonal seams, join assorted medium and dark print 2½×14" strips to make a pieced binding strip. Bind with pieced binding strip. (For details, see Complete the Quilt.)

at the crossroads

DESIGNER **KRIS KERRIGAN**
PHOTOGRAPHER **GREG SCHEIDEMANN**

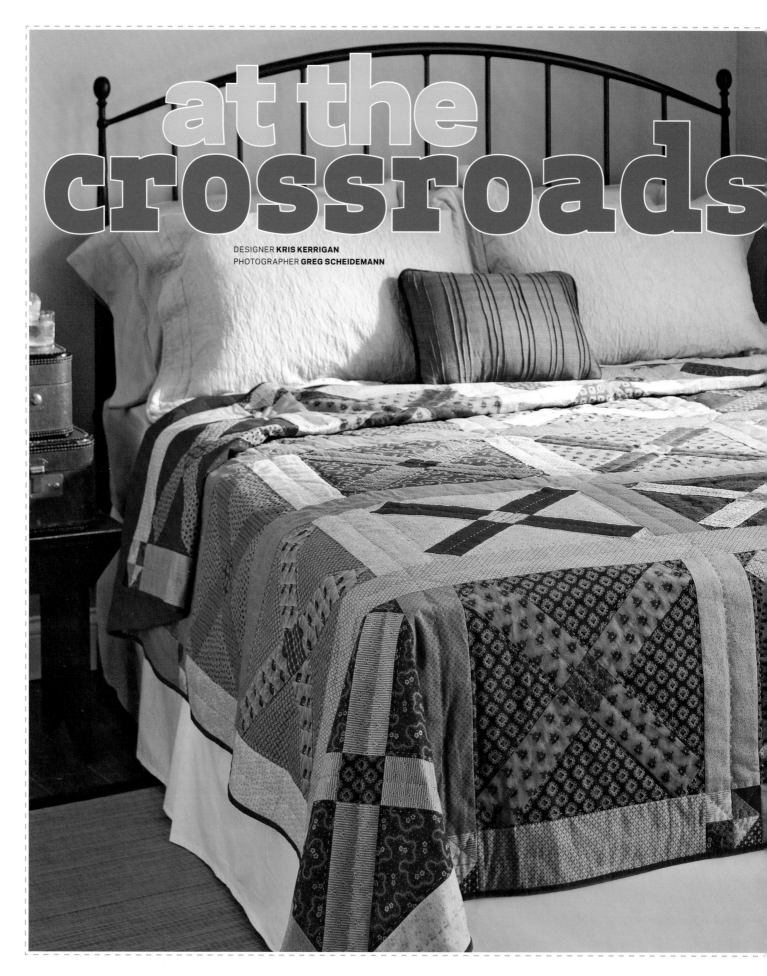

materials

When selecting assorted prints, choose pieces at least 12" square to have enough to cut triangles for the X blocks.

- 8¾ yards total assorted tan and gold prints (blocks, sashing)
- ⅞ yard red tone-on-tone (binding)
- 1¼ yards total assorted red prints (blocks)
- 2 yards total assorted blue prints (blocks)
- ⅝ yard total assorted green prints (blocks)
- ⅝ yard total assorted purple prints (blocks)
- ⅛ yard orange print (blocks)
- 8¼ yards backing fabric
- 99×116" batting
- 2 balls of perle cotton No. 8: taupe

Finished quilt: 92⅛×109¾"
Finished blocks: X block, 14⅛" square;
Broken Dishes block, 3½" square

Quantities are for 44/45"-wide, 100% cotton fabrics. Measurements include ¼" seam allowances. Sew with right sides together unless otherwise stated.

cut fabrics

Cut pieces in the order that follows in each section.

From assorted tan and gold prints, cut:
- 15—4×42" strips for sashing (5 sets of 3 matching pieces)
- 46—4×14⅝" sashing rectangles

From red tone-on-tone, cut:
- 11—2½×42" binding strips

An assortment of earthy colored fabrics combined in a graphic design results in a stunning, scrappy bed quilt.

cut and assemble X blocks

To give your quilt more interest, make some X blocks with dark and light prints for high contrast, while constructing other blocks with pieces of similar value for low contrast. Vary the position of dark and light prints to produce a scrappier appearance.

The following instructions make one X block. Repeat the cutting and assembly instructions to make 30 X blocks total.

DIAGRAM 1

DIAGRAM 2

From one assorted print, cut:
▸ 1—11⅞" square, cutting it diagonally twice in an X for 4 large triangles total
▸ 2—2⅝" squares, cutting each in half diagonally for 4 small triangles total

From a second print, cut:
▸ 4—3×8" rectangles

From a third print, cut:
▸ 1—3" square

[1] Referring to **Diagram 1**, sew together large triangles, rectangles, and square in three diagonal rows. Press seams toward rectangles. Join rows to make center unit. Press seams toward middle row.

[2] Sew a small triangle to a corner of center unit **(Diagram 2)**. Press seam toward center unit. Repeat with remaining small triangles to make an X block. The block should be 14⅝" square including seam allowances.

cut and assemble broken dishes blocks

For an optional assembly method, see Triangle-Squares Another Way on *page 91*.

From assorted tan and gold print scraps, cut:
▸ 44—2⅝" squares

From assorted print scraps, cut:
▸ 44—2⅝" squares

[1] Use a pencil to mark a diagonal line on wrong side of each tan and gold print 2⅝" square.

[2] Layer a marked square atop an assorted print 2⅝" square. Sew together with two seams, stitching ¼" on each side of drawn line **(Diagram 3)**.

[3] Cut pair apart on drawn line to make two triangle units **(Diagram 3)**. Open triangle units and press seams toward darker print to make two triangle-squares. Each triangle-square should be 2¼" square including seam allowances.

[4] Repeat steps 2 and 3 to make 88 triangle-squares total.

[5] Referring to **Diagram 4** for direction of seams, sew together four triangle-squares in pairs. Press seams in opposite directions. Join pairs to make a Broken Dishes block. Press seam to one side. The block should be 4" square including seam allowances. Repeat to make 22 Broken Dishes blocks total.

DIAGRAM 3

DIAGRAM 4

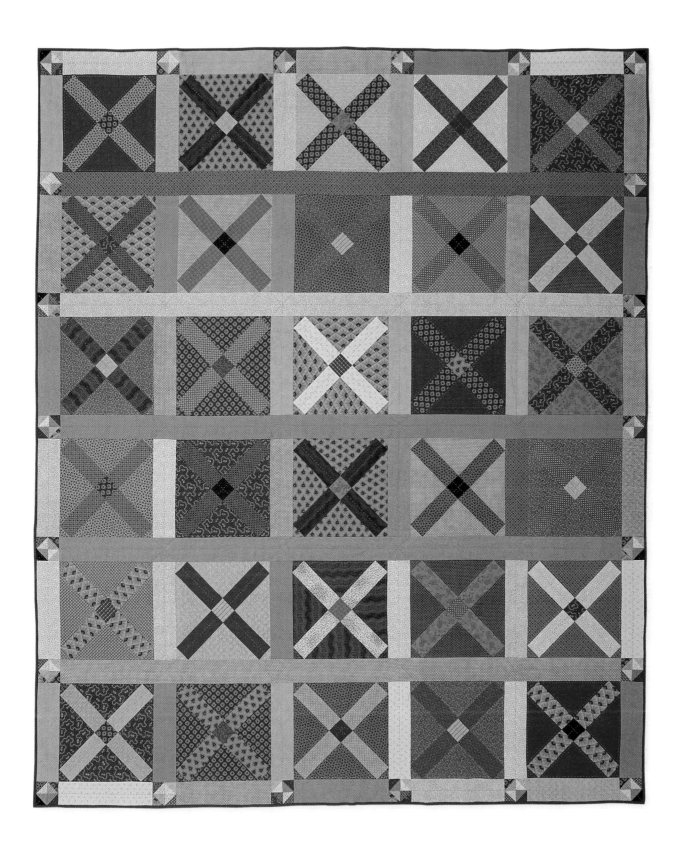

assemble quilt top

[1] Using matching tan and gold prints in each strip, cut and piece 4×42" strips to make:
▸ 5—4×85⅛" sashing strips

[2] Referring to **Quilt Assembly Diagram,** lay out Broken Dishes blocks, sashing rectangles, X blocks, and sashing strips in 13 rows.

[3] Sew together pieces in each row. Press seams toward sashing rectangles and sashing strips. Join rows to make quilt top. Press seams in one direction.

finish quilt

[1] Layer quilt top, batting, and backing; baste. (For details, see Complete the Quilt, *page 174.*)

[2] Quilt as desired. To achieve a primitive, folk art look, use taupe perle cotton No. 8 and a big stitch to hand-quilt an X in

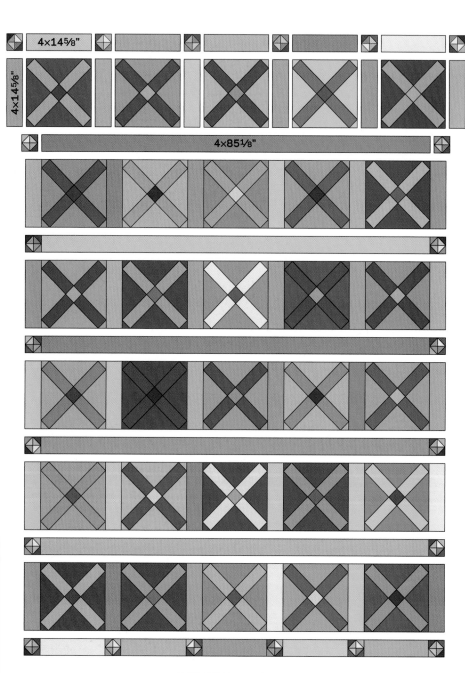

QUILT ASSEMBLY DIAGRAM

QUILTING DIAGRAM

each X block. Stitch ¼" from the seam line in the large triangles and in the middle of the sashing pieces **(Quilting Diagram).**

[3] Bind with red tone-on-tone binding strips. (For details, see Complete the Quilt.)

triangle-squares another way

Designer Kris Kerrigan offers an alternative method for making the triangle-squares needed for Broken Dishes blocks.

From assorted tan and gold print scraps, cut:
▸ 8—2⅝×15¾" rectangles
From assorted print scraps, cut:
▸ 8—2⅝×15¾" rectangles

1. On wrong side of each tan or gold print 2⅝×15¾" rectangle use a pencil to mark a horizontal line every 2⅝".

2. Referring to **Diagram 5**, use a pencil to mark a diagonal line in each 2⅝" section of all marked strips.
3. Layer each marked strip atop an assorted print strip. Sew ¼" on each side of diagonal lines.
4. Cut layered strips into squares on 2⅝" horizontal lines. Cut squares apart on diagonal lines to make 96 triangle units.
5. Open triangle units and press seams toward darker prints to make 96 triangle-squares (you will use 88).

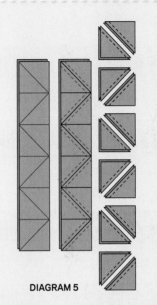

DIAGRAM 5

✹ COLOR OPTION ✹

Youthful fabrics and a tic-tac-toe-style setting give this nine-block version of At the Crossroads a game-board vibe. Take advantage of the X blocks' large rectangles to showcase fussy-cut designs and directional patterns. For a coordinated look, use leftovers from the larger blocks to make identical Broken Dishes blocks.

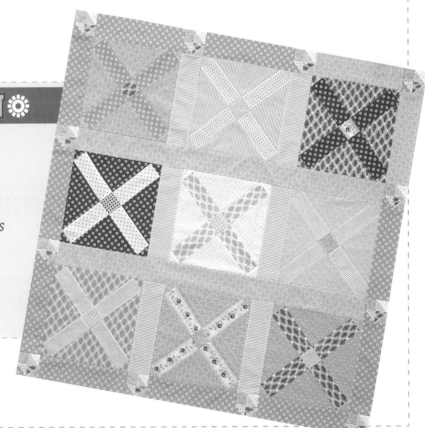

This seemingly complex quilt may turn heads, but putting it together won't leave you scratching yours. Take a closer look and you'll discover it's made of just two blocks: a star block in two colorways and an hourglass block that's rotated.

materials

- 2¾ yards total assorted red prints (blocks)
- 2¾ yards total assorted black prints (blocks)
- 3 yards total assorted cream and tan prints (blocks)
- ⅝ yard dark red print (inner border)
- 2⅛ yards black leaf print (outer border, binding)
- 7½ yards backing fabric
- 89×99" batting

Finished quilt: 82½×92½"
Finished blocks: 10" square

Quantities are for 44/45"-wide, 100% cotton fabrics.
Measurements include ¼" seam allowances. Sew with right sides together unless otherwise stated.

two-piece puzzle

DESIGNER **TARA LYNN DARR**
QUILTER **JULIE HOCRAFFER**
PHOTOGRAPHER **KATHRYN GAMBLE**

cut fabrics

Cut pieces in the following order.

From assorted red prints, cut:
- 56—2×7½" rectangles
- 14—5¼" squares
- 56—2×4½" rectangles
- 112—3⅜" squares

From assorted black prints, cut:
- 56—2×7½" rectangles
- 14—5¼" squares
- 56—2×4½" rectangles
- 112—3⅜" squares

From assorted cream and tan prints, cut:
- 224—3⅜" squares
- 224—2" squares

From dark red print, cut:
- 8—2×42" strips for inner border

From black leaf print, cut:
- 9—5×42" strips for outer border
- 9—2½×42" binding strips

assemble hourglass blocks

[1] Use a pencil to mark a diagonal line on wrong side of each assorted red print 5¼" square.

[2] Layer a marked red print square atop an assorted black print 5¼" square. Sew together with two seams, stitching ¼" on each

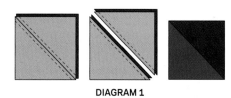

DIAGRAM 1

DIAGRAM 2

side of drawn line (Diagram 1). Cut apart on drawn line to make two triangle units. Press each triangle unit open, pressing seams toward black print, to make two red-and-black triangle-squares. Each triangle-square should be 4⅞" square including seam allowances. Repeat to make 28 red-and-black triangle-squares total.

[3] Use a pencil to mark a diagonal line on wrong side of 14 red-and-black triangle-squares, perpendicular to seam line (Diagram 2).

[4] Layer a marked triangle-square atop an unmarked red-and-black triangle-square, placing red print triangles on black print triangles (Diagram 2). Sew together with two seams, stitching ¼" on each side of drawn line. Cut apart on drawn line to make two triangle units. Press each unit open, pressing

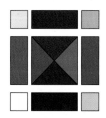

DIAGRAM 3

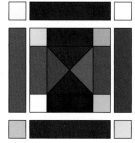

DIAGRAM 4

>> TIP <<

Measure your quilt center before cutting border strips. In the real world, things don't always come out as indicated in the instructions. If you stretch borders to make them fit, your quilt top will appear rippled or wavy.

seams in one direction, to make two hourglass units. Each hourglass unit should be 4½" square including seam allowances. Repeat to make 28 hourglass units total.

[5] Lay out an hourglass unit, two black print 2×4½" rectangles, two red print 2×4½" rectangles, and four assorted cream or tan print 2" squares in three rows (Diagram 3; note placement of black and red prints). Sew together pieces in each row. Press seams toward rectangles. Join rows to make a block center. Press seams away from center row. The block center should be 7½" square including seam allowances.

[6] Lay out the block center, two black print 2×7½" rectangles, two red print 2×7½" rectangles, and four assorted cream or tan print 2" squares in three rows (Diagram 4; again note placement of black and red prints). Sew together pieces in each row.

Press seams toward 2×7½" rectangles. Join rows to make an hourglass block. Press seams away from center row. The block should be 10½" square including seam allowances.

[7] Repeat steps 5 and 6 to make 28 hourglass blocks total.

assemble star blocks

[1] Use a pencil to mark a diagonal line on wrong side of each assorted cream and tan print 3⅜" square.

[2] Using marked cream and tan print squares and assorted red print 3⅜" squares, repeat Assemble Hourglass Blocks, Step 2, *page 94*, to make 224 red triangle-squares total (**Diagram 5**).

[3] Using remaining marked cream and tan print squares and assorted black print 3⅜"

squares, repeat Assemble Hourglass Blocks, Step 2, to make 224 black triangle-squares total (**Diagram 6**).

[4] Referring to **Diagram 7** for color placement, lay out eight red triangle-squares and eight black triangle-squares in four rows. Sew together pieces in each row. Press seams in one direction, alternating the direction with each row. Join rows to make Star Block A. Press seams in one direction. The block should be 10½" square including seam allowances. Repeat to make 12 total of Star Block A.

[5] Referring to **Diagram 8** for color placement, repeat Step 4 to make 16 of Star Block B.

assemble quilt top

[1] Referring to **Quilt Assembly Diagram,** lay out blocks in eight horizontal rows, rotating hourglass blocks and alternating A and B star blocks with each row.

[2] Sew together blocks in each row. Press seams toward hourglass blocks. Join rows to make quilt center. Press seams in one direction. The quilt center should be 70½×80½" including seam allowances.

[3] Cut and piece dark red print 2×42" strips to make:
  ‣ 2—2×80½" inner border strips
  ‣ 2—2×73½" inner border strips

DIAGRAM 5 DIAGRAM 6

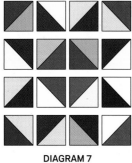

DIAGRAM 7
Star Block A

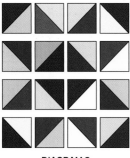

DIAGRAM 8
Star Block B

QUILTING DIAGRAM

[4] Sew long inner border strips to long edges of quilt center. Add short inner border strips to remaining edges. Press all seams toward inner border.

[5] Cut and piece black leaf print 5×42" strips to make:
  ‣ 2—5×83½" outer border strips
  ‣ 2—5×82½" outer border strips

[6] Sew long outer border strips to long edges of quilt center. Add short outer border strips to remaining edges to complete quilt top. Press all seams toward outer border.

finish quilt

[1] Layer quilt top, batting, and backing; baste. (To achieve an aged, puckered look, designer used cotton batting.) (For details, see Complete the Quilt, *page 174.*)

[2] Quilt as desired. The featured quilt was machine-quilted with a swirling heart design across the quilt top (Quilting Diagram).

[3] Bind with black leaf print binding strips. (For details, see Complete the Quilt.)

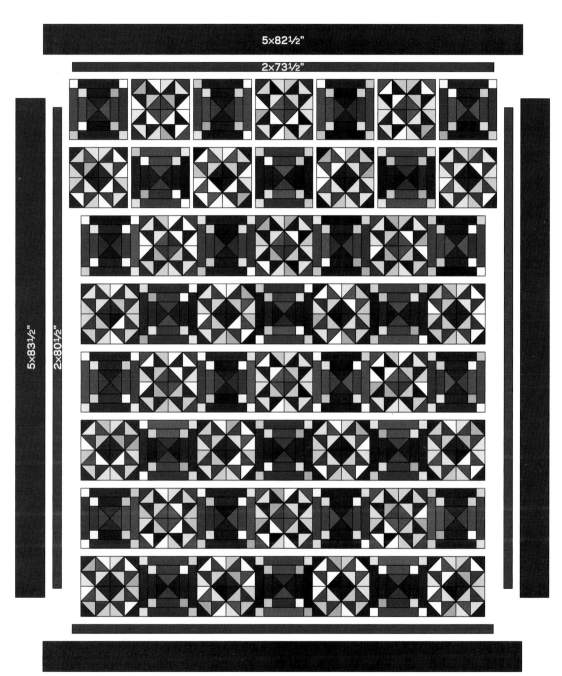

5×82½"

2×73½"

5×83½"

2×80½"

QUILT ASSEMBLY DIAGRAM

it's a treat

DESIGNER **LILA TAYLOR SCOTT**
PHOTOGRAPHERS **GREG SCHEIDEMANN** AND **MARTY BALDWIN**

materials

- ⅞ yard total assorted multicolor prints in purple, black, and green (blocks)
- 2¼ yards total assorted novelty prints (blocks)
- 1¼ yards total assorted orange prints (blocks)
- ⅝ yards total assorted yellow prints (blocks)
- 1 yard mottled purple (border, binding)
- 4 yards backing fabric
- 70" square batting

Finished quilt: 63½" square
Finished block: 12" square

Quantities are for 44/45"-wide, 100% cotton fabrics. Measurements include ¼" seam allowances. Sew with right sides together unless otherwise stated.

cut fabrics

Cut pieces in the following order.

From assorted multicolor prints, cut:

- 16—6⅞" squares, cutting each in half diagonally for 32 large triangles total

From assorted novelty prints, cut:

- 28—6⅞" squares, cutting each in half diagonally for 56 large triangles total
- 156—2⅞" squares, cutting each in half diagonally for 312 small triangles total (52 sets of six matching triangles)

From assorted orange prints, cut:

- 30—6⅞" squares, cutting each in half diagonally for 60 large triangles total

From assorted yellow prints, cut:

- 78—2⅞" squares, cutting each in half diagonally for 156 small triangles total (52 sets of three matching triangles)

From mottled purple, cut:

- 7—2½×42" binding strips
- 7—2×42" strips for border

assemble block A

[1] Sew together an assorted multicolor print large triangle and a novelty print large triangle to make a triangle-square (Diagram 1). Press seam open. The triangle-square should be 6½" square including seam allowances.

[2] Repeat Step 1 to make 32 triangle-squares total.

[3] Aligning edges of novelty print triangles, join four triangle-squares in pairs (Diagram 2). Press seams in opposite directions. Sew together pairs, with novelty prints in the center, to make a multicolor block A. Press seam open. Multicolor block A should be 12½" square including seam allowances.

[4] Repeat Step 3 to make eight multicolor A blocks total.

[5] Repeat steps 1 and 3 using eight orange print and eight novelty print large triangles to make two orange A blocks total.

DIAGRAM 1

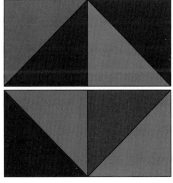

DIAGRAM 2

There's no trick to making this throw—just use your favorite Halloween novelty print scraps to make the contrasting light and dark blocks.

[6] Repeat steps 1 and 3 using 16 novelty print large triangles to make two novelty A blocks total.

assemble block B

[1] Referring to **Diagram 3**, lay out six matching novelty print small triangles and three matching yellow print small triangles in three rows.

[2] Sew together triangles in each row. Finger-press seams open. Join rows to make a triangle unit; gently press seams open as seams are on the bias.

[3] Sew together a triangle unit and an orange print large triangle to make a block B unit (**Diagram 4**). Press seam open. Block B unit should be 6½" square including seam allowances.

☼ COLOR OPTION ☼

Instead of novelty prints, choose florals and set them on black backgrounds to make this rich-looking table topper. By choosing fewer prints and repeating fabrics in the blocks, the quilt appears less scrappy and more formal.

[4] Repeat steps 1 through 3 to make 52 block B units total.

[5] Referring to **Diagram 5** for placement, sew together four block B units in pairs. Press seams in opposite directions. Join pairs to make block B. Press seam open. Block B should be 12½" square including seam allowances. Repeat to make 13 total of block B.

assemble quilt center

[1] Referring to **Quilt Assembly Diagram** for placement, lay out blocks in five rows, alternating A and B blocks. (The featured quilt was arranged with multicolor A blocks around edges of quilt center.)

[2] Sew together blocks in each row. Press seams in one direction, alternating direction with each row. Join rows to make quilt center. Press seams in one direction. The quilt center should be 60½" square including seam allowances.

add border

[1] Cut and piece mottled purple 2×42" strips to make:
  ‣ 2—2×63½" border strips
  ‣ 2—2×60½" border strips

[2] Sew short border strips to opposite edges of quilt center. Add long border strips to remaining edges. Press all seams toward border.

QUILT ASSEMBLY DIAGRAM

finish quilt

[1] Layer quilt top, batting, and backing; baste. (For details, see Complete the Quilt on *page 174*.)

[2] Quilt as desired. The featured quilt was machine-quilted with gold-metallic swirls and meandering stipples across the quilt.

[3] Bind with mottled purple binding strips. (For details, see Complete the Quilt.)

DIAGRAM 3

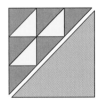

DIAGRAM 4

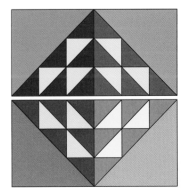

DIAGRAM 5

ROYAL
order

DESIGNER
JAN RAGALLER
QUILTER
ROBIN SAUNDERS
PHOTOGRAPHER
**CAMERON
SADEGHPOUR**

materials

- 6—¼-yard pieces assorted purple prints (blocks)
- 6—¼-yard pieces assorted red prints (blocks)
- 5—¼-yard pieces assorted gold prints (blocks)
- 5—¼-yard pieces assorted green prints (blocks)
- 2¼ yards tan tone-on-tone (blocks, sashing)
- 2⅝ yards dark purple print (sashing, inner and outer borders, binding)
- ⅜ yard red tone-on-tone (inner border)
- 4 yards backing fabric
- 72×83" batting

Finished quilt: 66×76½"
Finished blocks: 9" square

Quantities are for 44/45"-wide, 100% cotton fabric. Measurements include ¼" seam allowances. Sew with right sides together unless otherwise stated.

cut fabrics

Cut pieces in the following order.

From *each* assorted purple, red, gold, and green print, cut:
- 3—1½×42" strips

From tan tone-on-tone, cut:
- 71—2×9½" rectangles
- 30—3½" squares
- 240—2" squares

From dark purple print, cut:
- 8—5½×42" strips for outer border
- 8—2½×42" binding strips
- 42—2" sashing squares
- 336—1¼" squares

From red tone-on-tone, cut:
- 22—1¼×9½" strips
- 26—2×1¼" rectangles
- 4—1¼" squares

Set off a bevy of stars with richly colored, subtly pieced block backgrounds. Strip piecing combined with stitch-and-flip corners make the construction easier than you might think.

assemble rail fence units

[1] Join three different purple print 1½×42" strips to make a strip set (Diagram 1). Press seams in

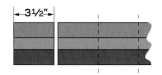

DIAGRAM 1

DIAGRAM 2

DIAGRAM 3

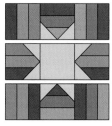

DIAGRAM 4

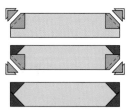

DIAGRAM 5

DIAGRAM 6

one direction. Repeat, mixing purple prints to achieve variety, to make six strip sets total. Cut strip sets into 64—3½"-wide purple Rail Fence units. Each unit should be 3½" square including seam allowances.

[2] Using assorted red print 1½×42" strips, repeat Step 1 to make 64 red Rail Fence units.

[3] Using assorted gold print 1½×42" strips, repeat Step 1 to make five strip sets, cutting them into 56 gold Rail Fence units.

[4] Using assorted green print 1½×42" strips, repeat Step 1 to make five strip sets, cutting them into 56 green Rail Fence units.

assemble blocks

[1] For one purple star block, gather eight purple Rail Fence units, one tan tone-on-tone 3½" square, and eight tan tone-on-tone 2" squares.

[2] Use a pencil to mark a diagonal line on wrong side of each tan tone-on-tone 2" square.

[3] Align a marked square with one corner of a Rail Fence unit (Diagram 2; note directions of marked line and Rail Fence seams). Sew on marked line; trim seam allowance to ¼". Press open attached triangle.

[4] Align a marked square with adjoining corner of Rail Fence unit (Diagram 2; again note directions of marked line and seams). Stitch, trim, and press

as before to make a vertical star point unit. The unit should be 3½" square including seam allowances.

[5] Repeat steps 3 and 4 to make a second vertical star point unit. Referring to Diagram 3, position Rail Fence seams horizontally and repeat steps 3 and 4 to make two horizontal star point units.

[6] Referring to Diagram 4 for placement, sew together remaining Rail Fence units, two vertical and two horizontal star point units, and tan tone-on-tone 3½" square in rows. Press seams away from star point units. Join rows to make a purple star block. Press seams in one direction. The star block should be 9½" square including seam allowances.

[7] Repeat steps 1–6 to make eight purple star blocks total.

[8] Using red, gold, and green Rail Fence units, repeat steps 1–6

to make eight red star blocks, seven gold star blocks, and seven green star blocks.

assemble sashing units

[**1**] Use a pencil to mark a diagonal line on wrong side of each dark purple print 1¼" square.

[**2**] Align marked dark purple print squares with two corners of a tan tone-on-tone 2×9½" rectangle (**Diagram 5**; note direction of marked lines). Stitch, trim, and press as in Assemble Blocks, Step 3.

[**3**] Repeat Step 2 to add marked dark purple print squares to remaining corners of Step 2 tan tone-on-tone rectangle to make a sashing unit (**Diagram 5**; again note direction of marked lines). The sashing unit should be 9½×2" including seam allowances.

[**4**] Repeat steps 2 and 3 to make 71 sashing units total. (Set aside remaining marked dark purple print 1¼" squares for inner border.)

assemble quilt center

[**1**] Referring to **Quilt Assembly Diagram** on *page 107*, lay out star blocks, sashing units, and dark purple print 2" sashing squares in 13 horizontal rows. Alternate the direction of the Rail Fence units in the star blocks as shown.

[**2**] Sew together pieces in each row. Press seams toward sashing units. Join rows to

make quilt center. Press seams toward block rows. The quilt center should be 54½×65" including seam allowances.

assemble and add borders

[**1**] Align a remaining marked dark purple print 1¼" square with one end of a red tone-on-tone 2×1¼" rectangle (**Diagram 6**;

note direction of marked line). Stitch, trim, and press as in Assemble Blocks, Step 3.

[**2**] Align a marked dark purple print square with opposite end of Step 1 red tone-on-tone rectangle (**Diagram 6**; again note direction of marked line). Stitch, trim, and press as before to make a Flying Geese unit. The unit should be 2×1¼" including seam allowances.

[3] Repeat steps 1 and 2 to make 26 Flying Geese units total.

[4] Referring to **Quilt Assembly Diagram,** sew together seven Flying Geese units and six red tone-on-tone 1¼×9½" strips to make a long inner border strip. Press seams toward red tone-on-tone strips. The long inner border strip should be 1¼×65" including seam allowances. Repeat to make a second long inner border strip.

[5] Join two red tone-on-tone 1¼" squares, six Flying Geese units, and five red tone-on-tone 1¼×9½" strips to make a short inner border strip. Press seams toward red tone-on-tone strips. The short inner border strip should be 1¼×56" including seam allowances. Repeat to make a second short inner border strip.

[6] Sew long inner border strips to long edges of quilt center. Sew short inner border strips to remaining edges. Press seams toward inner border.

[7] Cut and piece dark purple print 5½×42" strips to make:
  ‣ 2—5½×66½" outer border strips
  ‣ 2—5½×66" outer border strips

[8] Sew 5½×66½" outer border strips to long edges of quilt center. Add 5½×66" outer border strips to remaining edges to complete quilt top. Press all seams toward outer border.

finish quilt

[1] Layer backing, batting, and quilt top; baste. (For details, see Complete the Quilt, *page 174*)

[2] Quilt as desired. This version was machine-quilted with an eight-point motif in each tan tone-on-tone star and in each dark purple star formed by the sashing units **(Quilting Diagram).** The block

QUILTING DIAGRAM

backgrounds feature a feather design, and the outer border was stitched with a larger feather motif. The tan tone-on-tone portions of the sashing units were outline-quilted.

[3] Bind with dark purple print binding strips. (For details, see Complete the Quilt.)

❄ COLOR OPTION ❄

With chocolate brown stars in pieced cream backgrounds, this nine-block version of Royal Order features reversed placement of lights and darks. A blue ombré inner border and red print stars in the sashing pick up flecks of blue and red sprinkled throughout many of the brown prints.

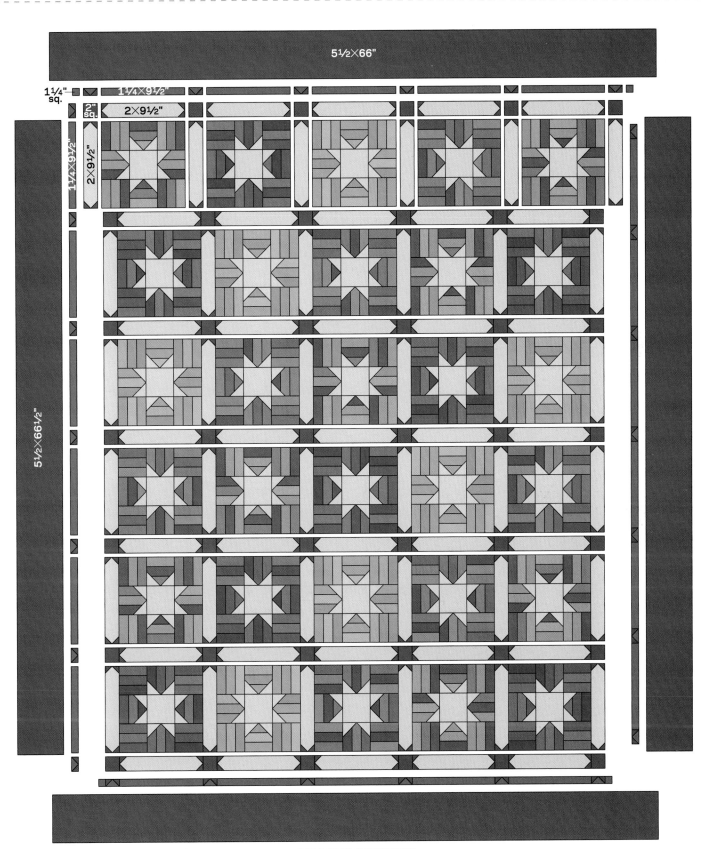

QUILT ASSEMBLY DIAGRAM

main event

DESIGNER **KATHIE HOLLAND** MACHINE QUILTER **MARY VAUGHAN** PHOTOGRAPHER **GREG SCHEIDEMANN**

materials

- 3½ yards total assorted medium and dark prints (pieced rows)
- 5⅛ yards red paisley (sashing, border, binding)
- 8¼ yards backing fabric
- 97×100" batting

Finished quilt: 90½×94"

Quantities are for 44/45"-wide, 100% cotton fabrics. Measurements include ¼" seam allowances. Sew with right sides together unless otherwise stated.

cut fabrics

Cut pieces in the following order. Cut sashing, border, and binding strips lengthwise (parallel to the selvages).

From assorted medium and dark prints, cut:
- 990—1½×3½" rectangles

From red paisley, cut:
- 2—9½×90½" border strips
- 10—4¾×90½" sashing strips
- 5—2½×85" binding strips

assemble pieced rows

Referring to **Quilt Assembly Diagram** on *page 110,* lay out 90 assorted print 1½×3½" rectangles in a row. Sew together rectangles to make a pieced row; press seams in one direction. The pieced row should be 3½×90½" including seam allowances. Repeat to make 11 pieced rows total.

Simple rectangles lend brilliant color to a stash-busting bed-size quilt. What could be easier?

>>TIP<<

To ease in a bit of extra fullness when the
lengths of two units don't quite match, sew with
the longer unit on the bottom against the machine bed.

assemble quilt top

[1] Referring to **Quilt Assembly Diagram**, lay out pieced rows, red paisley sashing strips, and red paisley border strips in 23 rows.

[2] Sew together rows and strips to make quilt top. Press seams in one direction.

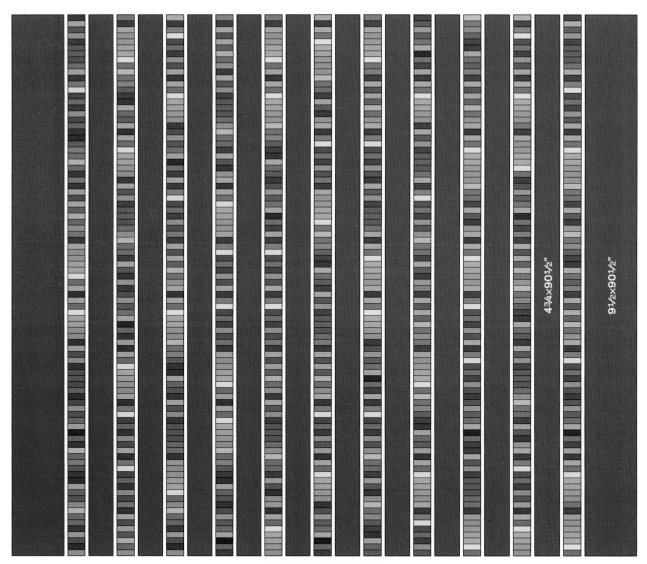

4³/₄×90¹/₂"

9¹/₂×90¹/₂"

QUILT ASSEMBLY DIAGRAM

finish quilt

[1] Layer quilt top, batting, and backing; baste. (For details, see Complete the Quilt, *page 174*.)

[2] Quilt as desired. The featured quilt was stitched with an allover free-form feather pattern.

[3] Bind with red paisley binding strips. (For details, see Complete the Quilt.)

designer notes

Kathie likes to have pre-cut strips on hand so she can start a project anytime. Whenever she finishes a project, she cuts her remaining fabric into assorted-width strips and stores them in stacking wire baskets that are clearly marked with the strip width. Over time, she collects an assortment that she can turn into a scrappy quilt top, pillow, or table runner.

❋ COLOR OPTION ❋

This pint-size version of The Main Event is perfect for a baby quilt or for a toddler to cuddle up with on a cool fall day.

To duplicate this 41×58½" quilt, choose a print for the sashing strips first, then select nine complementary prints for the small rectangles. When using fewer fabrics in the pieced rows, it's faster to sew long strips together into a strip set before cutting them into 3½"-wide units.

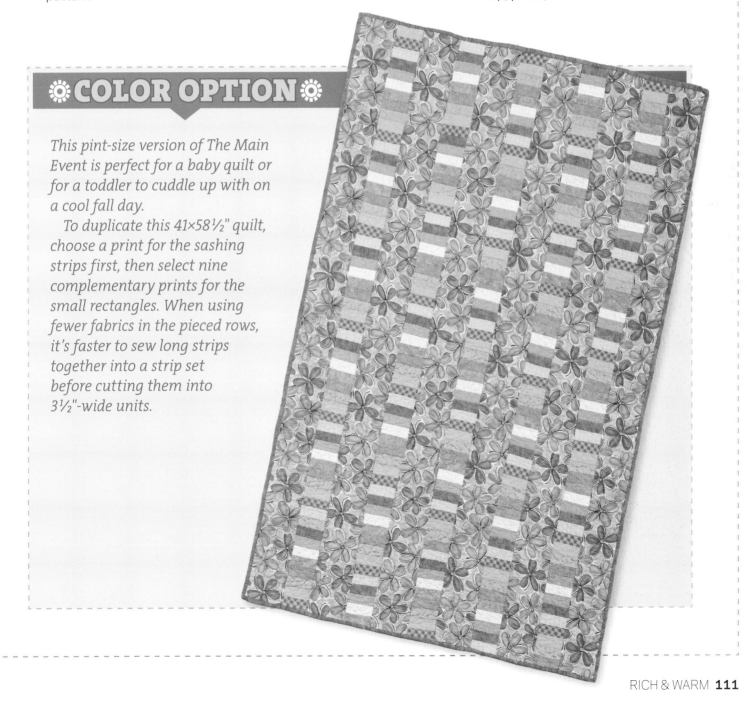

color rich

DESIGNER **MARY MCCARTHY** AND **PAM BUDA**
QUILTMAKER **JAN RAGALLER** QUILTER **CINDY TOLLIVER**
PHOTOGRAPHER **SCOTT LITTLE** AND **GREG SCHEIDEMANN**

Indulge in the rich colors of autumn with this scrappy quilt that takes its color cues from the fallen leaves of the season.

materials

- 4⅜ yards total assorted dark prints in orange, red, green, brown, and purple (blocks, outer border)
- 1⅓ yards total assorted light prints in cream and tan (blocks, outer border)
- 1⅜ yard black print (inner border, binding)
- 4 yards backing fabric
- 71×83" batting

Finished quilt: 64½×76½"
Finished block: 12" square

Quantities are for 44/45"-wide, 100% cotton fabrics. Measurements include ¼" seam allowances. Sew with right sides together unless otherwise stated.

cut fabrics

Cut pieces in the following order.

From assorted dark prints, cut:
- 80—6½" squares
- 48—3½" squares
- Enough 6½"-wide pieces in lengths ranging from 3½" to 12½" to total 210" for outer border

From assorted light prints, cut:
- 24—3½×6½" rectangles
- 80—3½" squares

From black print, cut:
- 6—2½×42" strips for inner border
- Enough 2½"-wide bias strips to total 300" for binding (For details, see Cutting Bias Strips on *page 174*.)

assemble blocks

[1] Mark a diagonal line on wrong side of each assorted light print 3½" square.

[2] Align a marked light print square with one corner of an assorted dark print 6½" square (**Diagram 1**; note direction of drawn line). Sew on drawn line; trim excess, leaving ¼" seam allowance.

[3] Press open attached triangle to make a block unit. The block unit should be 6½" square including seam allowances.

[4] Repeat steps 2 and 3 to make 80 block units total.

[5] Referring to **Diagram 2**, sew together four block units in pairs. Press seams in opposite directions. Join pairs to make a block. Press seam in one direction. The block should be 12½" square including seam allowances. Repeat to make 20 blocks total.

assemble quilt center

[1] Referring to **Quilt Assembly Diagram,** lay out 20 blocks in five rows.

[2] Sew together blocks in each row. Press seams in one direction, alternating direction with each row.

[3] Join rows to make quilt center. Press seams in one direction. The quilt center should be 48½×60½" including seam allowances.

≫TIP≪

The outer border in the featured quilt was pieced using 3½"-, 6½"-, 9½"-, and 12½"-long rectangles, all of them 6½" wide. However, if your scraps are a different size, feel free to mix up the lengths or add more Flying Geese units.

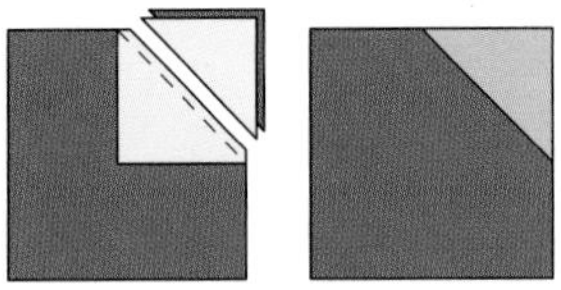

| DIAGRAM 1 | DIAGRAM 2 | DIAGRAM 3 |

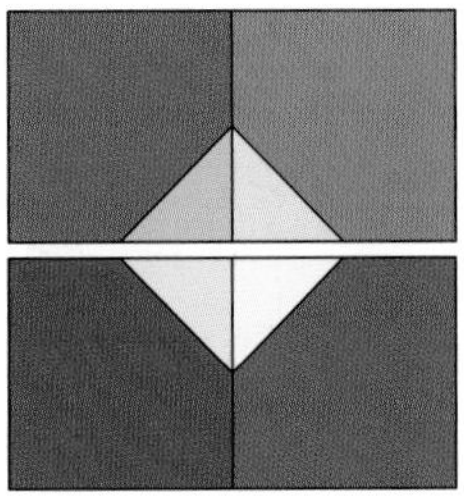

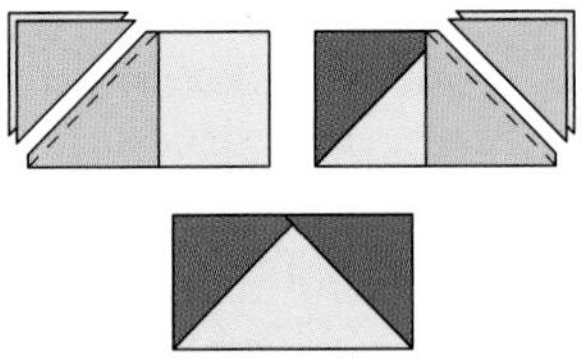

ALTERNATE QUILT SIZES	WALL	FULL/QUEEN	KING
Number of blocks	9	42	56
Number of blocks wide by long	3×3	6×7	7×8
Finished size	52½" square	88½×100½"	100½×112½"
Number of Flying Geese units	16	32	36
YARDAGE REQUIREMENTS			
Total assorted dark prints	2⅔ yards	7½ yards	9½ yards
Total assorted light prints	⅞ yard	2¼ yards	2¾ yards
Black print	1 yard	1⅝ yards	1⅝ yards
Backing	3⅓ yards	8 yards	8⅞ yards
Batting	59" square	95×107"	107×119"

OPTIONAL SIZE CHART

add inner border

[1] Cut and piece black print 2½×42" strips to make:
- ▸ 2—2½×60½" inner border strips
- ▸ 2—2½×52½" inner border strips

[2] Sew long inner border strips to long edges of quilt center. Add short inner border strips to remaining edges. Press all seams toward inner border.

assemble and add outer border

[1] Mark a diagonal line on wrong side of each assorted dark print 3½" square.

[2] Align a marked dark print square with one end of a light print 3½×6½" rectangle (**Diagram 3**; note direction of drawn line). Sew on drawn line; trim excess, leaving ¼" seam allowance. Press open attached triangle.

[3] Align and sew a second marked dark print square to opposite end of light print rectangle (**Diagram 3**; again note direction of drawn line). Trim and press as before to make a Flying Geese unit. The unit should be 3½×6½" including seam allowances.

[4] Repeat steps 2 and 3 to make 24 Flying Geese units total.

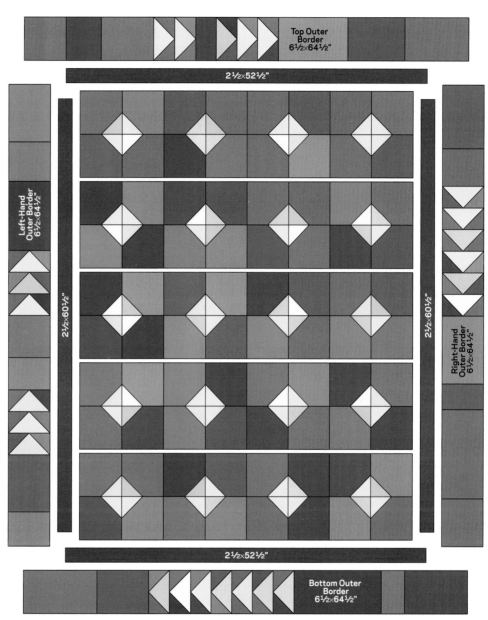

QUILT ASSEMBLY DIAGRAM

[5] Cut and piece assorted dark print 6½"-wide pieces and Flying Geese units to make:
- ▸ 1—6½×64½" right-hand outer border strip
- ▸ 1—6½×64½" left-hand outer border strip
- ▸ 1—6½×64½" bottom outer border strip
- ▸ 1—6½×64½" top outer border strip

[6] Sew outer border strips to side edges of quilt center (Quilt Assembly Diagram, *page 115*). Press seams toward outer border. Add remaining strips to top and bottom edges to complete quilt top; press as before.

finish quilt

[1] Layer quilt top, batting, and backing. (For details, see Complete the Quilt, *page 174*.)

[2] Quilt as desired. This quilt was machine-quilted with an allover stylized leaf pattern.

[3] Bind with black print binding strips. (For details, see Complete the Quilt.)

☼ COLOR OPTION ☼

Berry blues, creamy whites, and neutral tans combine in scrappy abundance for this version of Color Rich. If blue isn't your favorite color, choose a different hue as your primary color and select fabrics in a range of shades.

scattered leaves

DESIGNER **PAM BUDA**
QUILTER **RONDA DRANTER**
PHOTOGRAPHER **ADAM ALBRIGHT**

Add Log Cabin–like borders to adjoining edges of Maple Leaf units for pieced blocks that can be twisted and turned into a mazelike quilt. A scrappy assortment of dark and medium prints produces a cozy seasonal throw.

materials

- 1⅛ yards tan print (blocks)
- 8—18×22" pieces (fat quarters) assorted prints in gold, orange, red, brown, black, purple, green, and blue (leaf units, blocks)
- 3⅞ yards total assorted medium to dark prints, plaids, and stripes in gold, orange, red, brown, black, purple, green, and blue (blocks)
- 1¼ yards red leaf print (border)
- ⅔ yard green tone-on-tone (binding)
- 5 yards backing fabric
- 78×87" batting

Finished quilt: 71½×80½"
Finished block: 9" square

Quantities are for 44/45"-wide, 100% cotton fabrics. Measurements include ¼" seam allowances. Sew with right sides together unless otherwise stated.

cut fabrics

From tan print, cut:
- 56—2⅜" squares
- 168—2" squares
- 112—1½" squares

From _each_ of the 8 assorted print fat quarters, cut:
- 7—2×5" rectangles
- 7—2×3½" rectangles
- 7—2⅜" squares
- 7—2" squares

From scraps of assorted prints and from assorted medium to dark prints, plaids, and stripes, cut:
- 56—2×9½" rectangles
- 112—2×8" rectangles
- 112—2×6½" rectangles
- 56—2×5" rectangles

From red leaf print, cut:
- 8—4½×42" strips for border

From green tone-on-tone, cut:
- 8—2½×42" binding strips

assemble maple leaf units

[1] For one Maple Leaf unit, gather the following tan print pieces for the background: one 2⅜" square, three 2" squares, and two 1½" squares. Then pull the following pieces from one assorted print for the leaf: one 2⅜" square, one 2" square, one 2×3½" rectangle, and one 2×5" rectangle.

[2] Use a pencil to draw a diagonal line on wrong side of two of the tan print 2" squares and all tan print 2⅜" and 1½" squares.

[3] Layer marked tan print 2⅜" square atop the print 2⅜" square. Sew together with two seams, stitching ¼" on each side of drawn line (Diagram 1).

[4] Cut apart on drawn line to make two triangle units (Diagram 2). Press each triangle unit open, pressing seams toward darker print, to make two triangle-squares (Diagram 3). Each triangle-square should be 2" square including seam allowances.

[5] Align a marked tan print 2" square with one end of the print 2×5" rectangle (Diagram 4; note direction of marked line). Stitch on marked line; trim seam allowance to ¼". Press open attached triangle to make a long rectangle unit. The unit still should be 2×5" including seam allowances.

[6] Align a marked tan print 2" square with one end of the print 2×3½" rectangle (Diagram 5; again note direction of marked line). Stitch, trim, and press as before to make a short rectangle unit. The unit still should be 2×3½" including seam allowances.

[7] Align marked tan print 1½" squares with opposite corners of the print 2" square (Diagram 6). Stitch, trim, and press as before to make a stem unit. The stem unit still should be 2" square including seam allowances.

[8] Referring to Diagram 7, lay out the two triangle-squares, long and short rectangle units, stem unit, and remaining tan print 2" square in three rows. Join pieces in each row; press seams in one direction. Join rows to make a Maple Leaf unit. Press seams in one direction. The leaf unit should be 5" square including seam allowances.

[9] Repeat steps 1–8 to make 56 Maple Leaf units total.

DIAGRAM 1

DIAGRAM 2

DIAGRAM 3

DIAGRAM 4

DIAGRAM 5

DIAGRAM 6

DIAGRAM 7

≫ TIP ≪

"To reduce fabric-cutting time but still end up with a scrappy quilt, I asked two friends to make the same quilt. We each made blocks in matching sets of three and traded them, auditioning fabrics from our stashes first to ensure they played well together." — DESIGNER PAM BUDA

assemble blocks

[1] Referring to **Diagram 8**, sew an assorted print, plaid, or stripe 2×5" rectangle to right-hand edge of a Maple Leaf unit. Press seam away from Maple Leaf unit. Add an assorted print, plaid, or stripe 2×6½" rectangle to bottom edge. Press as before.

[2] Referring to **Diagram 9**, add four more assorted print, plaid, or stripe rectangles to Step 1 Maple Leaf unit to make a block. Press all seams away from Maple Leaf unit. The block should be 9½" square including seam allowances.

[3] Repeat steps 1 and 2 to make 56 blocks total.

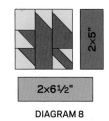

2×6½"

DIAGRAM 8

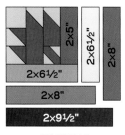

2×5"

2×6½"

2×8"

2×6½"

2×8"

2×9½"

DIAGRAM 9

assemble quilt center

[1] Referring to **Quilt Assembly Diagram**, lay out blocks in eight horizontal rows, paying attention to the direction each leaf is pointing.

[2] Sew together blocks in each row. Press seams in one direction, alternating direction with each row.

[3] Join rows to make quilt center. Press seams in one direction. The quilt center should be 63½×72½" including seam allowances.

❂ COLOR OPTION ❂

It's an autumn evening in this 35×44" version of Scattered Leaves. Each leaf, made from a single warm color, stands out from its low-contrast, neutral-tone frame. High-textured fabrics add even more interest.

4½x71½"

4½x72½"

QUILT ASSEMBLY DIAGRAM

add border

[1] Cut and piece red leaf print 4½×42" strips to make:
- 2—4½×72½" border strips
- 2—4½×71½" border strips

[2] Sew long border strips to long edges of quilt center. Add short border strips to remaining edges to complete quilt top. Press seams toward border.

finish quilt

[1] Layer quilt top, batting, and backing; baste. (For details, see Complete the Quilt, *page 174*.)

[2] Quilt as desired. This quilt features machine-quilting in an allover swirling leaf design across the quilt top (**Quilting Diagram**).

[3] Bind with green tone-on-tone binding strips. (For details, see Complete the Quilt.)

QUILTING DIAGRAM

>> **TIP** <<

Choose a single unifying background fabric for your leaf blocks to give the viewer's eye a place to rest in this scrappy quilt.

OPTIONAL SIZE CHART

ALTERNATE QUILT SIZES	CRIB/LAP	FULL/QUEEN	KING
Number of blocks	20	90	110
Number of blocks wide by long	4×5	9×10	10×11
Finished size	44½×53½"	89½×98½"	98½×107½"
YARDAGE REQUIREMENTS			
Tan print	½ yard	1⅔ yards	2 yards
Assorted prints	5 fat quarters or ¾ yard total	13 fat quarters or 2¼ yards total	16 fat quarters or 2⅔ yards total
Assorted medium to dark prints, plaids, and stripes	1½ yards total	5⅞ yards total	7⅛ yards total
Red leaf print	⅞ yard	1½ yards	1⅝ yards
Green tone-on-tone	½ yard	⅞ yard	⅞ yard
Backing fabric	2⅞ yards	8 yards	8¾ yards
Batting	51×60"	96×105"	105×114"

modern makeover

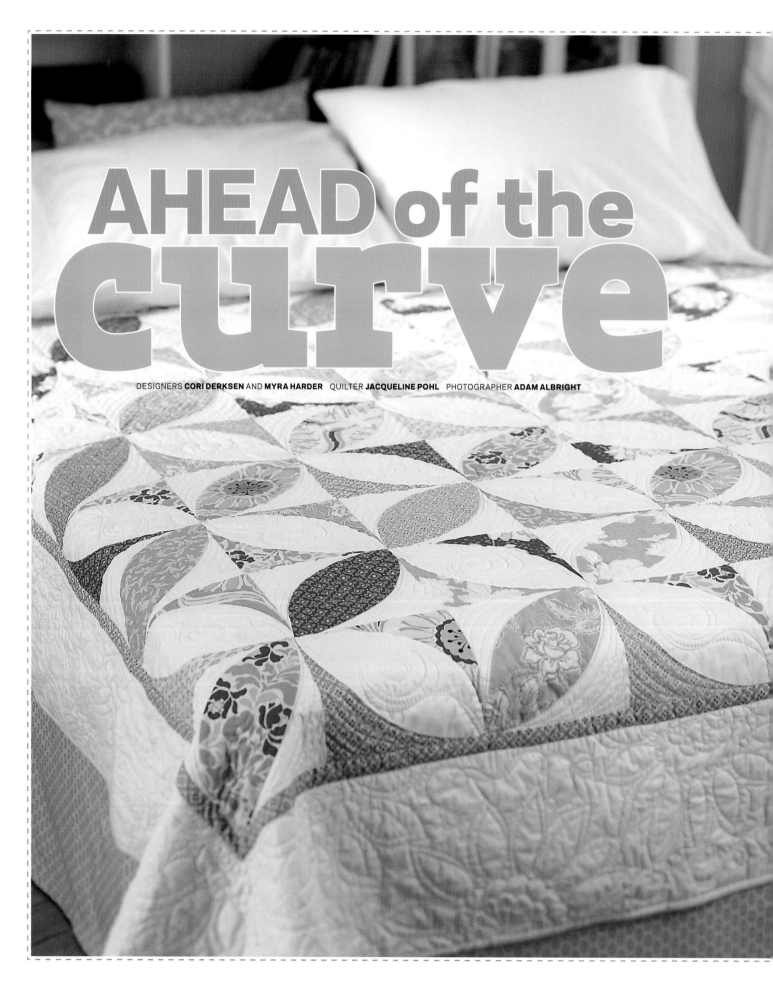

AHEAD of the curve

DESIGNERS **CORI DERKSEN** AND **MYRA HARDER**   QUILTER **JACQUELINE POHL**   PHOTOGRAPHER **ADAM ALBRIGHT**

materials

- 12—⅓-yard pieces assorted prints in red, green, aqua, and gold (blocks)
- 7 yards solid white (blocks, outer border, binding)
- ½ yard aqua print (inner border)
- 7⅔ yards backing fabric
- 92×108" batting

Finished quilt: 85½×101½"
Finished block: 16" square

Quantities are for 44/45"-wide, 100% cotton fabric. Measurements include ¼" seam allowances. Sew with right sides together unless otherwise stated.

cut fabrics

Cut pieces in the following order.

The patterns are on *Pattern Sheet 2*. To make templates of patterns, see Make and Use Templates, *page 170*. Be sure to transfer dots to templates, then to fabric pieces. These dots are matching points and are necessary when joining pieces.

Cut outer border strips lengthwise (parallel to the selvages).

From assorted prints, cut:
- 80 of Pattern A
- 40 of Pattern B

From solid white, cut:
- 2—10×85½" outer border strips
- 2—10×82½" outer border strips
- 10—2½×42" binding strips
- 80 of Pattern A
- 40 of Pattern B

From aqua print, cut:
- 8—1½×42" strips for inner border

Add a new technique to your skill set by learning to piece curved seams with ease. Bold prints and bright white combine to make a stunning bed quilt.

assemble A units

When joining pieces, be sure to align marked matching points. To do this, push a pin through center of dots on layered pieces.

[1] Layer a solid white B piece atop an assorted print A piece; match center dots on curved edges (Diagram 1).

[2] Using slender pins and picking up only a few threads at a time, pin at center, ends, and remaining dots, then generously in between (Diagram 2).

[3] Join pieces, removing each pin just before your needle reaches it. Press seam toward A piece (Diagram 3).

[4] Repeat steps 1–3 to add a second assorted print A piece to opposite edge of B piece to make a Unit A (Diagram 4). Press as before. Unit A should be 8½" square including seam allowances.

[5] Repeat steps 1–4 to make 40 A units total.

assemble B units

[1] Layer an assorted print B piece atop a solid white A piece; match center dots on curved edges. Repeat Assemble A Units, steps 2 and 3.

[2] Repeat Step 1 to add a second solid white A piece to opposite edge of B piece to make a Unit B (Diagram 5). Press seam toward A piece just added. Unit B should be 8½" square including seam allowances.

[3] Repeat steps 1 and 2 to make 40 B units total.

tips for piecing curves perfectly

  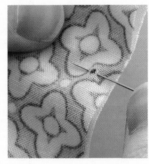 

1) To ease curved fabric pieces together for pinning, hold the piece with the convex edge (B in this project) on top of the piece with the concave edge (A).

2) If desired, make small clips into the seam allowance of the concave edge (the edge that curves in), but do not cut into or beyond the seam lines. Do not clip the convex edge.

3) Align dots on A and B pieces by pushing a pin through them. *(The pushing pin has been omitted from this photo for clarity.)* Using a second pin, pick up a few threads and pin pieces together. Remove first pin.

4) Ease the A piece along the gentle curve of the B piece and make sure you haven't pinned in any folds or tucks. When sewing together the pieces, sew slowly and remove each pin as your needle reaches it.

DIAGRAM 1

DIAGRAM 2

DIAGRAM 3

UNIT A
DIAGRAM 4

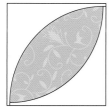

UNIT B
DIAGRAM 5

assemble blocks

[1] Referring to **Diagram 6**, pair two A units and two B units. Sew together units in each pair. Press seams toward A units.

[2] Join pairs to make a Melon Patch block. Press seam in one direction. The block should be 16½" square.

[3] Repeat steps 1 and 2 to make 20 Melon Patch blocks total.

assemble quilt center

[1] Referring to **Quilt Assembly Diagram,** lay out blocks in five rows. Sew together blocks in each row. Press seams in one direction, alternating the direction with each row.

[2] Join rows to make quilt center. Press seams in one direction. The quilt center should be 64½×80½" including seam allowances.

add borders

[1] Cut and piece aqua print 1½×42" strips to make:
- ▸ 2—1½×80½" inner border strips
- ▸ 2—1½×66½" inner border strips

[2] Sew long inner border strips to long edges of quilt center. Add short inner border strips to remaining edges. Press all seams toward inner border.

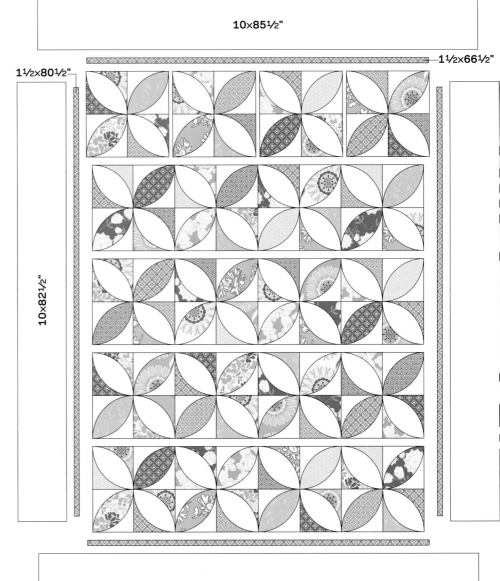

10×85½"

1½×66½"

1½×80½"

10×82½"

QUILT ASSEMBLY DIAGRAM

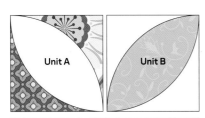

Unit A   Unit B

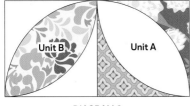

Unit B   Unit A

DIAGRAM 6

[3] Sew solid white 10×82½" outer border strips to long edges of quilt center. Add solid white 10×85½" outer border strips to remaining edges to complete quilt top. Press all seams toward inner border.

finish quilt

[1] Layer quilt top, batting, and backing; baste. (For details, see Complete the Quilt, *page 174*.)

[2] Quilt as desired. The featured quilt was machine-quilted with a swirling design in the B pieces, echo-quilting in the A pieces, and a floral design in the outer border (**Quilting Diagram**).

[3] Bind with solid white binding strips. (For details, see Complete the Quilt.)

>> TIP <<

"A wide white border is the perfect place to showcase custom quilting."
—DESIGNER MYRA HARDER

QUILTING DIAGRAM

ALTERNATE QUILT SIZES	THROW	TWIN	KING
Number of blocks	9	8	25
Number of blocks wide by long	3×3	2×4	5×5
Number of A and B units	18	16	50
Finished size	69½" square	53½×85½"	101½" square
YARDAGE REQUIREMENTS			
Assorted prints	7—⅓-yard pieces	6—⅓-yard pieces	15—⅓-yard pieces
Solid white	4⅔ yards	4¼ yards	8⅝ yards
Aqua print	⅓ yard	⅓ yard	½ yard
Backing fabric	4¼ yards	5⅛ yards	9 yards
Batting	76" square	60×92"	108" square

OPTIONAL SIZE CHART

my guy

DESIGNERS **BILL KERR AND WEEKS RINGLE**
PHOTOGRAPHER **GREG SCHEIDEMANN**

materials

- 8—18×22" pieces (fat quarters) assorted plaids and stripes in blue, gray, and brown (blocks)
- 4¼ yards solid brown (blocks, border, binding)
- 5⅛ yards backing fabric
- 61×92" batting

Finished quilt: 54½×85½"
Finished block: 9×4"

Quantities are for 44/45"-wide, 100% cotton fabric. Measurements include ¼" seam allowances. Sew with right sides together unless otherwise stated.

cut fabrics

Cut pieces in the following order. Cut border strips lengthwise (parallel to the selvages).

From assorted plaids and stripes, cut:
- 188—2×5" rectangles

From solid brown, cut:
- 8—2½×42" binding strips
- 2—5×76½" border strips
- 2—5×54½" border strips
- 48—4½×9½" setting rectangles
- 47—1½×9½" rectangles

»TIP«

Yarn-dyed stripes and plaids tend to be looser weaves than most quilting cottons and may get distorted when washed and dried. To prepare them for cutting, press the fabric well; use a little spray starch if needed to help the fabric lie flat.

It's not always easy to find a quilt pattern that suits your guy's simple style. Here's a not-too-fussy way to show him you care.

pressing method

Designers Bill Kerr and Weeks Ringle press all seams open to achieve a crisp, flat look.

"Pressing seams open also allows us to precisely align seams and easily pin through them for accurate sewing," Bill says. You may choose to press all seams open or follow the pressing instructions included in each assembly step.

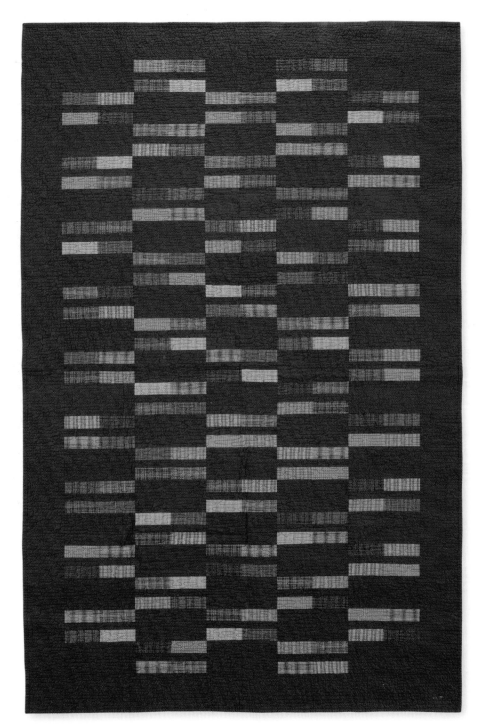

assemble blocks

[1] Aligning short ends, sew together two assorted plaid and stripe 2×5" rectangles to make a rectangle pair (Diagram 1). Press seam in one direction. Repeat to make 94 rectangle pairs total.

[2] Referring to Diagram 2, sew rectangle pairs to long edges of a solid brown 1½×9½" rectangle to make a block. Press seams toward solid brown rectangle. The block should be 9½×4½" including seam allowances. Repeat to make 47 blocks total.

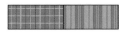

DIAGRAM 1

1½x9½"

DIAGRAM 2

≫ TIP ≪

"Be careful that no two of the same plaid or stripe are touching. Evenly distribute the most eye-catching fabrics throughout the entire quilt." —WEEKS RINGLE

assemble quilt top

[1] Referring to **Quilt Assembly Diagram**, lay out blocks and solid brown setting rectangles in vertical rows, alternating blocks and setting rectangles.

[2] Sew together pieces in each row. Press seams toward setting rectangles. Each pieced row should be $9\frac{1}{2} \times 76\frac{1}{2}"$ including seam allowances.

[3] Join rows to make quilt center. Press seams in one direction. The quilt center should be $45\frac{1}{2} \times 76\frac{1}{2}"$ including seam allowances.

[4] Sew long solid brown border strips to long edges of quilt center. Add short solid brown border strips to remaining edges to complete quilt top. Press all seams toward border.

finish quilt

[1] Layer quilt top, batting, and backing; baste. (For details, see Complete the Quilt, *page 174*.)

[2] Quilt as desired. Bill and Weeks machine-quilted an allover horizontal meander that accentuates the shape of the pieced strips. **(Quilting Diagram)**.

[3] Bind with solid brown binding strips. (For details, see Complete the Quilt.)

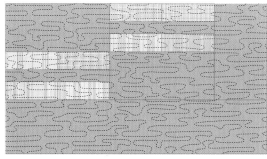

QUILTING DIAGRAM

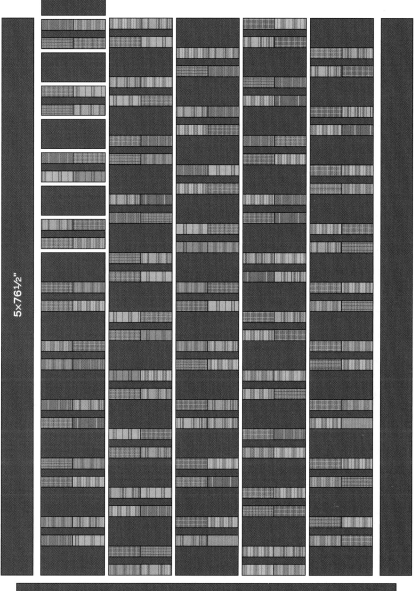

5×54½"

5×76½"

QUILT ASSEMBLY DIAGRAM

spice is nice

DESIGNER **MONICA SOLORIO-SNOW**
PHOTOGRAPHER **GREG SCHEIDEMANN**

Turn squares into hourglass units with an easy-to-sew, no-triangles technique.

materials

- 2¼ yards solid white (blocks)
- 1½ yards total assorted red, green, brown, and yellow prints (blocks)
- ⅔ yard green print (blocks)
- ¾ yard red-orange print (blocks)
- ½ yard yellow print (blocks)
- ½ yard multicolor stripe (inner border)
- 1½ yards red-orange floral (outer border)
- ¾ yard green geometric (binding)
- 5½ yards backing fabric
- 79×95" batting

Finished quilt: 72½×88½"
Finished block: 12" square

Quantities are for 44/45"-wide, 100% cotton fabrics. Measurements include ¼" seam allowances. Sew with right sides together unless otherwise stated.

cut fabrics

Cut pieces in the following order.

From solid white, cut:
- 64—5¼" squares
- 6—4½×12½" rectangles
- 8—4½×8½" rectangles
- 26—4½" squares

From assorted red, green, brown, and yellow prints, cut:
- 97—4½" squares

From green print, cut:
- 32—5¼" squares

From red-orange print, cut:
- 20—5¼" squares

From yellow print, cut:
- 12—5¼" squares

From multicolor stripe, cut:
- 8—1½×42" strips for middle border

From red-orange floral, cut:
- 8—5½×42" strips for outer border

From green geometric, cut:
- 9—2½×42" binding strips

assemble hourglass units

[1] Use a pencil to mark two diagonal lines on wrong side of each solid white 5¼" square. (To prevent fabric from stretching as you draw the lines, place 220-grit sandpaper under each square.)

[2] Layer two marked solid white squares atop two green print 5¼" squares. Sew each pair together with two seams, stitching ¼" on each side of one drawn line (Diagram 1). Cut each pair apart on drawn line to make two triangle units. Press each triangle unit open, pressing seam toward green print, to make four triangle-squares total. Each triangle-square should be 4⅞" square including seam allowances.

[3] Layer two matching triangle-squares, placing green triangle atop solid white triangle. Extend diagonal line corner to corner from solid white to print fabric. Sew pair together ¼" on each side of drawn line (Diagram 2). Cut apart on drawn line to make two green hourglass units. Press each unit open, pressing seam in one direction. The hourglass unit should be 4½" square including seam allowances. Repeat with remaining two green-and-white triangle-squares.

DIAGRAM 1

DIAGRAM 2

[4] Repeat steps 2 and 3 to make 64 green hourglass units total.

[5] Using red-orange print and yellow print 5¼" squares, and remaining marked solid white 5¼" squares, repeat steps 2 and 3 to make 40 red hourglass units and 24 yellow hourglass units total.

assemble star blocks

[1] Referring to Diagram 3, lay out four red hourglass units and five assorted print 4½" squares.

[2] Sew together the pieces in rows. Press seams toward squares. Join rows to make a star block; press seams in one direction. The star block should be 12½" square including seam allowances.

[3] Referring to Quilt Assembly Diagram and photo (page 140), repeat steps 1 and 2 to make 10 red star blocks and two green star blocks total.

assemble sashing units

[1] For one vertical sashing unit, you'll need two hourglass units and one assorted print 4½" square.

[2] Sew hourglass units to opposite edges of the print 4½" square to make a vertical sashing unit. Press seams toward square. The vertical sashing unit should be 4½×12½" including seam allowances.

[3] Referring to Quilt Assembly Diagram, repeat steps 1 and 2 to make eight vertical sashing units total.

[4] For one horizontal sashing row, you'll need six hourglass units and five assorted print 4½" squares.

DIAGRAM 3

QUILT ASSEMBLY DIAGRAM

[5] Lay out hourglass units and print squares in a row, beginning and ending with a green hourglass unit (Quilt Assembly Diagram). Join to make a horizontal sashing row. The horizontal sashing row should be 4½×44½" including seam allowances.

[6] Referring to Quilt Assembly Diagram, repeat steps 4 and 5 to make three horizontal sashing rows total.

assemble quilt center

[1] Referring to Quilt Assembly Diagram, lay out 12 star blocks, eight vertical sashing units, and three horizontal sashing rows in seven horizontal rows.

[2] Sew together pieces in each block row. Press seams toward sashing units.

[3] Join rows to make quilt center. Press seams toward sashing rows. The quilt center should be 44½×60½" including seam allowances.

assemble and add inner border

[1] Referring to Quilt Assembly Diagram for top inner border strip, lay out three solid white 4½×12½" rectangles, five solid white 4½" squares, 12 green hourglass units, and four assorted print 4½" squares in two rows.

[2] Sew together pieces in each row. Join rows to make a top inner border strip. The top inner border strip should be 8½×60½" including seam allowances.

[3] Repeat steps 1 and 2 to make a bottom inner border strip.

[4] Referring to Quilt Assembly Diagram for side inner border strip, lay out four solid white 4½×8½" rectangles, eight solid white 4½" squares, 11 green hourglass units, and three assorted print 4½" squares.

[5] Sew squares and hourglass units in pairs. Join pairs to solid white rectangles to make a side inner border strip. The side inner border strip should measure 8½×60½" including seam allowances.

[6] Repeat steps 4 and 5 to make two side inner border strips total.

[7] Sew side inner border strips to side edges of quilt center. Sew top and bottom inner border strips to remaining edges. Press all seams toward border.

assemble and add middle and outer borders

[1] Cut and piece multicolor stripe 1½×42" strips to make:
  ‣ 2—1½×76½" middle border strips
  ‣ 2—1½×62½" middle border strips

[2] Sew long inner border strips to long edges of quilt center. Add short inner border strips to remaining edges. Press all seams toward inner border.

[3] Cut and piece red-orange floral 5½×42" strips to make:
  ‣ 2—5½×78½" outer border strips
  ‣ 2—5½×72½" outer border strips

[4] Sew long outer border strips to long edges of quilt center. Add short outer border strips to remaining edges to complete quilt top. Press all seams toward outer border.

finish quilt

[1] Layer quilt top, batting, and backing; baste. (For details, see Complete the Quilt, *page 174*.)

[2] Quilt as desired. The machine-quilted pebble pattern that was stitched across the entire quilt

top of this version of Spice is Nice was stitched with yellow thread.

[3] Bind with green geometric binding strips. (For details, see Complete the Quilt.)

DESIGNER **KEVIN KOSBAB**   QUILTER **HEATHER KOSBAB**
PHOTOGRAPHS **ADAM ALBRIGHT**

DOT to DOT

Intimidated by appliqué? Don't be! The gently curved edges of large circles make this a simple-to-sew quilt.

materials

- 3 yards total assorted solids in green and aqua (blocks)
- 3 yards total assorted prints in green, aqua, and blue (blocks)
- ⅝ yard aqua stripe (binding)
- 3⅛ yards backing fabric
- 55×79" batting
- Freezer paper
- Spray starch
- Clear monofilament polyester or nylon thread

Finished quilt: 48½x72½"
Finished blocks: 12" square

Quantities are for 44/45"-wide, 100% cotton fabric. Measurements include ¼" seam allowances. Sew with right sides together unless otherwise stated.

cut fabrics

Cut pieces in the following order. Patterns are on *Pattern Sheet 2*. To make a full Large Circle pattern, fold a sheet of paper in half. Trace pattern with its dotted line on the fold, cut out, and unfold.

To make templates and cut and prepare circle appliqués, see Prepare Appliqués, right.

From assorted solids, cut:
- 6—12½" squares
- 24—6½" squares
- 6 of Large Circle pattern
- 24 of Small Circle pattern

From assorted prints, cut:
- 6—12½" squares
- 24—6½" squares
- 6 of Large Circle pattern
- 24 of Small Circle pattern

From aqua stripe, cut:
- 7—2½x42" binding strips

prepare appliqués

The quilt shown was made using a freezer-paper-and-starch method for appliquéing. Instructions that follow are for this method.

[1] Lay freezer paper shiny side down over patterns. Use a pencil to trace each pattern the number of times indicated in cutting instructions, leaving ½" between tracings.

[2] Place each sheet of drawn circles shiny side down on a second sheet of freezer paper, also shiny side down. (Templates made with two layers of freezer paper have a sturdier edge, making it easier to turn under seam allowances.) Fuse together with a hot, dry iron. (If desired, use a nonstick pressing cloth so freezer paper won't adhere to the ironing board.) Cut out layered circles on drawn lines to make freezer-paper templates.

[3] Using a hot, dry iron, press a freezer-paper template shiny side down onto wrong side of designated fabric; let cool. Cut out fabric circle, adding a scant ¼" seam allowance to edge **(Diagram 1)**.

pattern play

When making Dot to Dot, designer Kevin Kosbab scouted quilt stores and dove into his stash for just the right fabrics. "I looked for prints that had flowers, starbursts, and spirograph-type motifs to complement the circular shape of the appliqué pieces," Kevin says. "Because the prints are graphic, I paired them with solids to ensure the circle shapes are still the focal point." To give the quilt more energy, he used several shades of green and aqua solids.

[**4**] Spray a small amount of spray starch into a dish or the starch bottle cap. Place a template-topped circle on pressing surface that is covered with a tea towel or muslin. Dip a small paintbrush or cotton swab into starch and moisten seam allowance of fabric circle (**Diagram 2**).

[**5**] Using the tip of a hot, dry iron, turn seam allowance over edge of freezer-paper template. Ensuring fabric is taut against template, press until fabric is dry. Press entire seam allowance in this manner, adding starch as necessary. Carefully peel off template to complete preparation of appliqué shape.

[**6**] Using fabrics indicated in cutting instructions, repeat steps 3–5 to prepare all large and small circles.

appliqué and make blocks

[**1**] Center a solid large circle on a print 12½" square (**Diagram 3**). Baste in place.

[**2**] With clear monofilament thread and a blind-hem stitch, machine-appliqué around circle to make an A block.

[**3**] Using remaining assorted solid large circles and assorted print 12½" squares, repeat steps 1 and 2 to make six A blocks total.

DIAGRAM 1

DIAGRAM 2

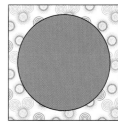

DIAGRAM 3

DIAGRAM 4

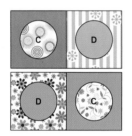

Unit C
DIAGRAM 5

Unit D
DIAGRAM 6

C   D

D   C

DIAGRAM 7

QUILTING DIAGRAM

[4] Using assorted print large circles and assorted solid 12½" squares, repeat steps 1 and 2 to make six B blocks **(Diagram 4)**.

[5] Position a print small circle on a solid 6½" square; baste in place **(Diagram 5)**. Machine-appliqué as before to make Unit C. Repeat to make 24 total of Unit C.

[6] Using assorted solid small circles and assorted print 6½" squares, repeat Step 5 to make Unit D **(Diagram 6)**. Repeat to make 24 total of Unit D.

☼ COLOR OPTION ☼

In just a day you can stitch up this six-block quilt for a budding paleontologist. A dash of black and white unifies bright novelty prints to make a great kid-size throw.

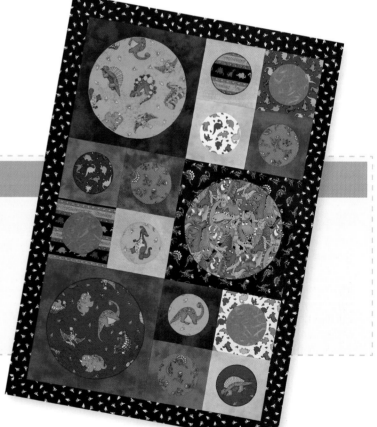

[7] Referring to **Diagram 7,** sew together two Unit Cs and two Unit Ds in pairs. Press seams toward Unit Cs. Join pairs to make a Four-Patch block. Press seam in one direction. The block should be 12½" square including seam allowances. Repeat to make 12 Four-Patch blocks total.

assemble quilt top

[1] Referring to **Quilt Assembly Diagram** for placement, lay out A, B, and Four-Patch blocks in six rows. Note that the Four-Patch blocks in the second, fourth, and sixth rows are rotated so that Unit Ds are in top left-hand corners.

[2] Sew together blocks in each row. Press seams in one direction, alternating direction with each row. Join rows to make quilt top. Press seams in one direction.

finish quilt

[1] Layer backing, batting, and quilt top; baste. (For details, see Complete the Quilt, *page 174*.)

[2] Quilt as desired. A variety of spirograph-inspired motifs were machine-quilted in the circle appliqués of this version of Dot to Dot **(Quilting Diagram).** A stipple design was also stitched in the background of the quilt top. Full-size quilting designs used in some of the small circle appliqués are on *Pattern Sheet 2.*

[3] Bind with aqua stripe binding strips. (For details, see Complete the Quilt.)

QUILT ASSEMBLY DIAGRAM

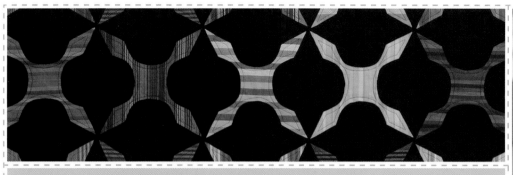

Black fabric sets off the scrappy striped appliqués that strut across this bold piece.

materials

- 7⅞ yards total assorted stripes (appliqués)
- 8⅛ yards solid black (appliqué foundations)
- ⅞ yard dark stripe (binding)
- 7¾ yards backing fabric
- 91×101" batting
- 24 yards lightweight fusible web
- Clear monofilament thread
- Template plastic

Finished quilt: 84½×95"
Finished block: 10½" square

Quantities are for 44/45"-wide, 100% cotton fabrics. Measurements include ¼" seam allowances. Sew with right sides together unless otherwise stated.

cut fabrics

To make the best use of your fabrics, cut pieces in the following order. The Four-Points pattern is on *Pattern Sheet 2*. To make a template of the pattern, see Make and Use Templates on *page 170*. Referring to **Template Diagram**, use a permanent marking pen to trace pattern four times onto template plastic, rotating pattern at dashed fold lines to form a square in the center. Do not cut out template.

To use fusible web for appliquéing, complete the following steps.

[1] Lay fusible web, paper side up, over pattern template. Use a pencil to trace pattern, including fold lines, 72 times, leaving ½" between tracings. Cut out each fusible-web shape roughly ¼" outside traced lines.

[2] Following the manufacturer's instructions, press fusible-web shapes onto wrong sides of assorted stripes; let cool. Cut out fabric shapes on drawn lines. Finger-press at fold lines and peel off paper backings.

From assorted stripes, cut:
- 72 of Four-Points pattern

From solid black, cut:
- 72—11½" squares

From dark stripe, cut:
- 10—2½×42" binding strips

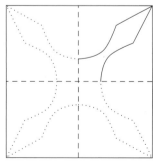

TEMPLATE DIAGRAM

QUILTMAKER **LAURA BOEHNKE**
QUILTER **SUE URICH**
PHOTOGRAPHER **ANDY LYONS**

color
BLAST

appliqué blocks

[1] Fold a solid black 11½" square in half twice. Lightly finger-crease folds to create a foundation square with appliqué placement guidelines; unfold (**Appliqué Placement Diagram**).

[2] Using folds as a guide, fuse a striped Four-Points piece to foundation square. Using clear monofilament thread and a zigzag stitch, machine-appliqué piece in place to make an appliquéd block. Trim block to 11" square, centering appliqué.

[3] Repeat steps 1 and 2 to make 72 appliquéd blocks total.

assemble quilt top

[1] Referring to **Quilt Assembly Diagram**, lay out appliquéd blocks in nine horizontal rows, alternating direction of striped appliqués.

[2] Sew together blocks in each row. Press seams in one direction, alternating direction with each row. Join rows to make quilt top. Press seams in one direction.

finish quilt

[1] Layer quilt top, batting, and backing; baste. (For details, see Complete the Quilt, *page 174*.)

[2] Quilt as desired. Each appliqué on the shown quilt was outline-quilted with black thread. The black background was stitched with wide crosshatching.

[3] Bind with dark stripe binding strips. (For details, see Complete the Quilt.)

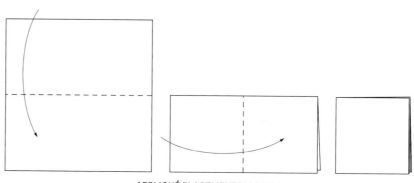

APPLIQUÉ PLACEMENT DIAGRAM

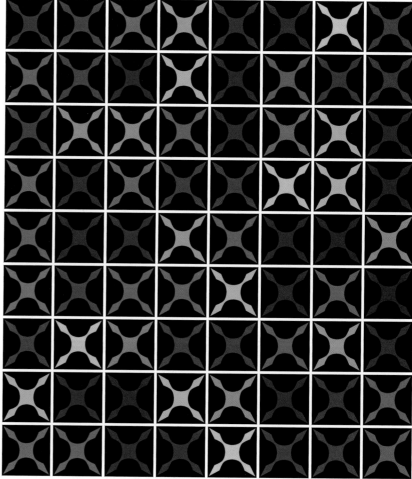

QUILT ASSEMBLY DIAGRAM

star struck

DESIGNER **BECKY GOLDSMITH**   QUILTMAKER **KATE HARDY**   QUILTER **LEANNE OLSON**   PHOTOGRAPHER **SCOTT LITTLE**

The traditional Dolly Madison's Star block comes alive with an energizing assortment of striped prints.

materials

- 2⅛ yards total of assorted dark prints in pink, orange, green, blue, and purple (blocks and border)
- 1⅜ yards total assorted light prints in pink, yellow, green, blue, and purple (blocks)
- 1½ yards white print (blocks)
- ⅝ yard multicolor stripe (binding)
- 3⅔ yards backing fabric
- 66" square of quilt batting

Finished quilt top: 60" square
Finished block: 18" square

Quantities are for 44/45"-wide, 100% cotton fabrics. Measurements include a ¼" seam allowance. Sew with right sides together unless otherwise stated.

cut the fabrics

To make the best use of your fabrics, cut the pieces in the order that follows.

From assorted dark prints, cut:
- 12—3½×18½" rectangles for border
- 4—3½" squares for border corners
- 126—3" squares, cutting each in half diagonally for a total of 252 small triangles
- 45—2½" squares

From assorted light prints, cut:
- 9—7¼" squares, cutting each diagonally twice in an X for a total of 36 large triangles
- 90—3" squares, cutting each in half diagonally for a total of 180 small triangles
- 36—2½" squares

From white print, cut:
- 36—6½" squares

From multicolor stripe, cut:
- 7—2½×42" binding strips

assemble the nine-patch units

[1] Referring to **Diagram 1**, lay out five dark print 2½" squares and four light print 2½" squares in three rows.

[2] Sew together the pieces in each row. Press the seam allowances toward the dark print squares. Then join the rows to make a Nine-Patch unit; press the seam allowances in one direction. The Nine-Patch unit should measure 6½" square, including the seam allowances.

[3] Repeat steps 1 and 2 to make a total of nine Nine-Patch units.

DIAGRAM 1

assemble the star point units

[1] Join a dark print small triangle and a light print small triangle to make a triangle-square (see **Diagram 2**). Press the seam allowance toward the dark print triangle. The pieced triangle-square should measure 2⅝" square, including the seam allowances. Repeat to make a total of 108 triangle-squares.

[2] Referring to **Diagram 3** for placement, lay out a triangle-square and two assorted light print small triangles. Join the pieces to make a light triangle unit. Press the seam allowances toward the triangle-square. Repeat to make a total of 36 light triangle units.

  Note: The long edge of each triangle unit is on the bias, so avoid stretching it out of shape while sewing.

[3] Referring to **Diagram 4**, lay out a triangle-square and two assorted dark print small triangles. Join the pieces to make a dark triangle unit. Press the seam allowances toward

DIAGRAM 2

DIAGRAM 3

DIAGRAM 4

DIAGRAM 5

the dark print triangles. Repeat to make a total of 72 dark triangle units.

[4] Referring to **Diagram 5**, lay out one light triangle unit, two dark triangle units, and a light print large triangle. Sew together the pieces in pairs. Press the seam allowances in opposite directions. Then join the pairs to make a star point unit. Press the seam allowance in one direction. The pieced star point unit should measure 6½" square, including the seam allowances. Repeat to make a total of 36 star point units.

DIAGRAM 6

assemble the blocks

[1] Referring to **Diagram 6**, lay out four star point units, four light print 6½" squares, and one Nine-Patch unit in three rows.

[2] Sew together the pieces in each row. Press the seam allowances toward the light print squares or Nine-Patch unit. Then join the rows to make a Dolly Madison's Star block. Press the seam allowances in one direction. The pieced block should measure 18½" square, including the seam allowances.

≫ TIP ≪

When determining which prints to use in a block, use a design wall to lay out your pieces and help simplify color placement. Even though the quilt is scrappy, you can bring "controlled" order to the quilt by making each Dolly Madison's Star block in primarily one or two colors.

[3] Repeat steps 1 and 2 to make a total of nine Dolly Madison's Star blocks.

assemble the quilt top

[1] Referring to the photograph for placement, lay out the nine star blocks in three horizontal rows. Sew together the blocks in each row. Press the seam allowances in one direction, alternating the direction with each row.

[2] Join the rows to complete the quilt center. Press the seam allowances in one direction. The pieced quilt center should measure 54½" square, including the seam allowances.

assemble and add the border

[1] Referring to the photograph, piece the dark print 3½×18½" rectangles to make the following:
   ‣ 4—3½×54½" border strips

[2] Sew pieced border strips to opposite edges of the pieced quilt center. Sew dark print 3½" squares to both ends of the remaining pieced border strips. Add these pieced border strips to the remaining edges of the pieced quilt center to complete the quilt top. Press all seam allowances toward the border.

complete the quilt

[1] Layer the quilt top, batting, and backing. (For details, see Complete the Quilt, *page 174.*

[2] Quilt as desired. The featured quilt was machine-quilted with an allover swirl pattern with varying swirls, stripes, and zigzags on each border segment. The corners were quilted with stars and swirls.

[3] Use the multicolor stripe 2½×42" strips to bind the quilt (For details, see Complete the Quilt.)

save the blues

DESIGNER **LEAH ANDERSON**
PHOTOGRAPHER **GREG SCHEIDEMANN**

Put your worn-out jeans to good use in this simple throw. Big-stitching detail adds a bright punch.

materials

- 9 pairs of jeans (blocks)
- ⅔ yard hot pink batik (binding)
- 3¾ yards backing fabric
- 66×76" batting
- Yarn: bulky-weight fuchsia, worsted-weight hot pink and silver metallic

Finished quilt: 60½×70½"
Finished blocks: 10" square; 10×20" rectangle

Quantities are for 44/45"-wide, 100% cotton fabrics. Measurements include a ¼" seam allowance. Sew with right sides together unless otherwise stated.

fabric notes

All jeans are not created equal; therefore, jeans in different sizes will yield different amounts of denim. Although the number of jeans you use will depend on their sizes, the nine pairs called for in the materials list should yield enough denim and color variations to make an eye-catching throw. To add the most contrast to the quilt top, be sure to include a variety of washes in the finished blocks.

cut fabrics

To make the best use of your fabrics, cut pieces in the following order.

Use cutting and assembly instructions that follow, or work with denim scraps cut from your jeans to create 42 blocks that are each 10½" square.

To get her denim scraps, designer Leah Anderson cut most pairs of jeans slightly to the left of the inside seam all the way up on one leg and slightly to the left of the outside seam all the way up on the other.

To get more texture and some fun detail in her blocks, Leah left

the jeans seam attached when measuring some of the denim pieces.

From jeans, cut:
- 2—6½x20½" rectangles
- 2—5½x20½" rectangles
- 2—4½x20½" rectangles
- 18—10½" squares
- 2—8½x10½" rectangles
- 3—7½x10½" rectangles
- 5—6½x10½" rectangles
- 5—5½x10½" rectangles
- 9—4½x10½" rectangles
- 5—3½x10½" rectangles
- 6—2½x10½" rectangles
- 4—5½x6½" rectangles
- 2—5½" squares
- 4—4½x5½" rectangles

From hot pink batik, cut:
- 7—2½x42" binding strips

assemble blocks

[1] Sew together a 6½x20½" rectangle and a 4½x20½" rectangle to make Block A **(Diagram 1)**. Press seam in one direction. Block A should be 10½x20½" including seam allowances. Repeat to make a second Block A.

>> TIP <<

To sew through denim, use a size 100/16 jeans/denim needle in your machine and adjust the stitch length to 3.0 mm.

[2] Join two 5½x20½" rectangles to make Block B **(Diagram 2)**. Press seam in one direction. Block B should be 10½x20½" including seam allowances.

[3] Sew together an 8½x10½" rectangle and a 2½x10½" rectangle to make Block C **(Diagram 3)**. Press seam in one direction. Block C should be 10½" square including seam allowances. Repeat to make a second Block C.

[4] Join a 7½x10½" rectangle and a 3½x10½" rectangle to make Block D **(Diagram 4)**. Press

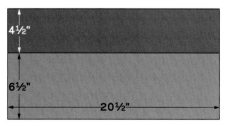

DIAGRAM 1 - BLOCK A

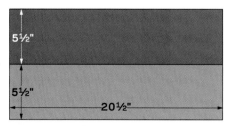

DIAGRAM 2 - BLOCK B

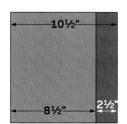

DIAGRAM 3 - BLOCK C

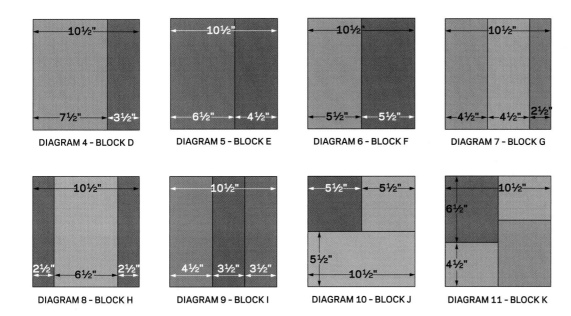

10½"				
7½"	3½"			

DIAGRAM 4 - BLOCK D

10½"
6½" 4½"

DIAGRAM 5 - BLOCK E

10½"
5½" 5½"

DIAGRAM 6 - BLOCK F

10½"
4½" 4½" 2½"

DIAGRAM 7 - BLOCK G

10½"
2½" 6½" 2½"

DIAGRAM 8 - BLOCK H

10½"
4½" 3½" 3½"

DIAGRAM 9 - BLOCK I

5½" 5½"
5½" 10½"

DIAGRAM 10 - BLOCK J

10½"
6½" 4½"

DIAGRAM 11 - BLOCK K

seam in one direction. Block D should be 10½" square including seam allowances. Repeat to make three total of Block D.

[5] Sew together a 6½×10½" rectangle and a 4½×10½" rectangle to make Block E (Diagram 5). Press seam in one direction. Block E should be 10½" square including seam allowances. Repeat to make four total of Block E.

[6] Join two 5½×10½" rectangles to make Block F (Diagram 6). Press seam in one direction. Block F should be 10½" square including seam allowances. Repeat to make a second Block F.

[7] Referring to Diagram 7, sew together two 4½×10½" rectangles and a 2½×10½" rectangle to make Block G. Press seams in one direction. Block G should be 10½" square including seam allowances. Repeat to make a second Block G.

[8] Referring to Diagram 8, join a 6½×10½" rectangle and two 2½×10½" rectangles to make Block H. Press seams in one direction. Block H should be 10½" square including seam allowances.

[9] Referring to Diagram 9, sew together a 4½×10½" rectangle and two 3½×10½" rectangles to make Block I. Press seams in one direction.

Block I should be 10½" square including seam allowances.

[10] Sew together two 5½" squares; press seam in one direction. Add a 5½×10½" rectangle to make Block J (Diagram 10). Press seam in one direction. Block J should be 10½" square including seam allowances.

[11] Referring to Diagram 11, sew together two 5½×6½" rectangles and two 4½×5½" rectangles in pairs. Press seams in opposite directions. Join pairs to make Block K; press seam in one direction. Block K should be 10½" square including seam allowances. Repeat to make a second Block K.

assemble quilt top

[1] Referring to **Quilt Assembly Diagram,** lay out the eighteen 10½" squares and the blocks in five horizontal rows.

[2] Sew together pieces in sections in the top and bottom rows. Press seams in one direction, alternating direction with each row. Join rows to make the quilt top. Press seams in one direction.

finish quilt

[1] Layer quilt top, batting, and backing; baste. (For details, see Complete the Quilt, *page 174.*)

[2] Quilt as desired. The quilt shown was hand-quilted with wavy lines across the quilt top using a running stitch and a backstitch with three colors and two weights of yarn for variety and texture.

To make a running stitch, pull needle up at A (see diagram *right*) and insert it back into fabric at B, about ¾" from A. Continue in same manner, leaving about a stitch width between each stitch.

To backstitch, pull needle up at A (see diagram bottom *right*). Insert it back into fabric at B (about ¾" from A), and bring it up at C. Push needle down again at D, and bring it up at E. Continue in same manner.

[3] Bind with hot pink batik binding strips. (For details, see Complete the Quilt.)

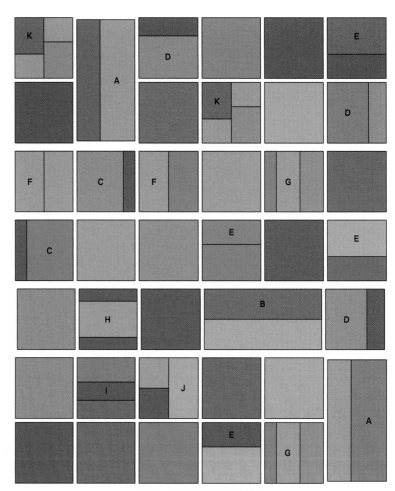

QUILT ASSEMBLY DIAGRAM

>> **TIP** <<

Press heavy denim seams open to reduce bulk. When quilting, use a rubber jar-lid opener to help pull the needle through the fabric layers.

RUNNING STITCH

BACKSTITCH

☼ COLOR OPTION ☼

This collection of Far-East fabrics heightens the contrast to Save the Blues. To duplicate this look, select fabrics from a single fabric collection. With more than a dozen complementary prints to choose from, you can make the quilt top as organized or as scrappy as you like.

sun-drenched strips

DESIGNER **PIECE O' CAKE DESIGNS**
QUILTER **MARY C. COVEY**
PHOTOGRAPHS **GREG SCHEIDEMANN**

materials

▸ 13—9×22" pieces (fat eighths) assorted bright solids (blocks)
▸ 1⅓ yards turquoise floral (sashing strips, border)
▸ ½ yard brown floral (binding)
▸ 2⅝ yards backing fabric
▸ 46×58" batting

Finished quilt: 39½×51½"

Quantities are for 44/45"-wide, 100% cotton fabrics. Measurements include ¼" seam allowances. Sew with right sides together unless otherwise stated.

cut fabrics

Cut pieces in the following order.

From each assorted bright solid, cut:
▸ 6—2×5½" rectangles
From turquoise floral, cut:
▸ 6—6½×39½" strips
From brown floral, cut:
▸ 5—2½×42" binding strips

assemble rows

Referring to **Quilt Assembly Diagram** on *page 163*, lay out two each of the 13 bright solid 2×5½" rectangles; sew together along long edges to make a row. Press seams in one direction. The row should be 5½×39½" including seam allowances. Repeat to make three rows total.

Mix up bars of saturated colors to form a striking counterpoint to a single floral fabric.

QUILTING DIAGRAM

assemble quilt top

[1] Referring to **Quilt Assembly Diagram,** join rows and four turquoise floral 6½×39½" strips. Press seams in one direction.

[2] Add remaining turquoise floral 6½×39½" strips to remaining edges to complete quilt top.

finish quilt

[1] Layer quilt top, batting, and backing; baste. (For details, see Complete the Quilt, *page 174.*)

[2] Quilt as desired. This quilt features a free-form palm leaf pattern in each row and floral strip **(Quilting Diagram).**

[3] Bind with brown floral binding strips. (For details, see Complete the Quilt.)

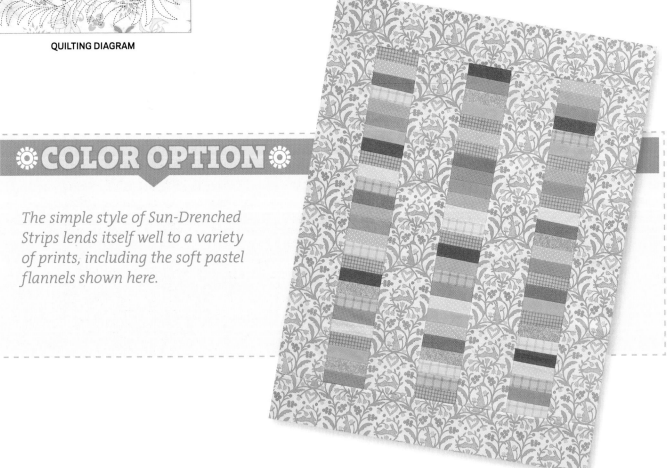

❂ COLOR OPTION ❂

The simple style of Sun-Drenched Strips lends itself well to a variety of prints, including the soft pastel flannels shown here.

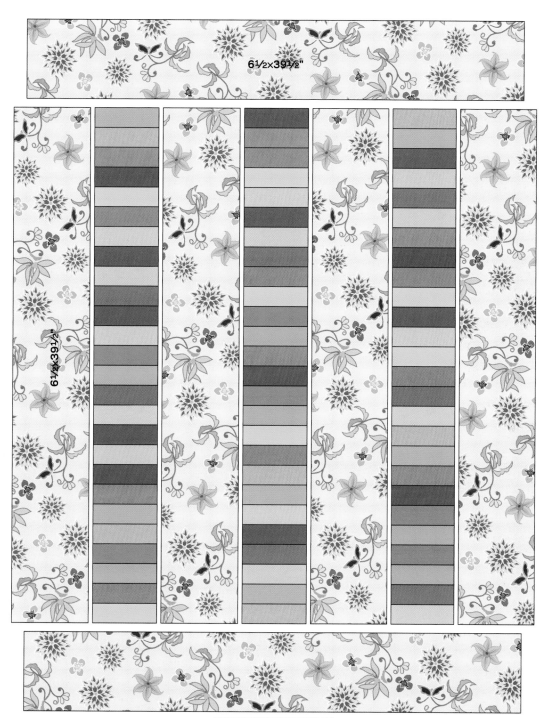

6½x39½"

6½x39½"

QUILT ASSEMBLY DIAGRAM

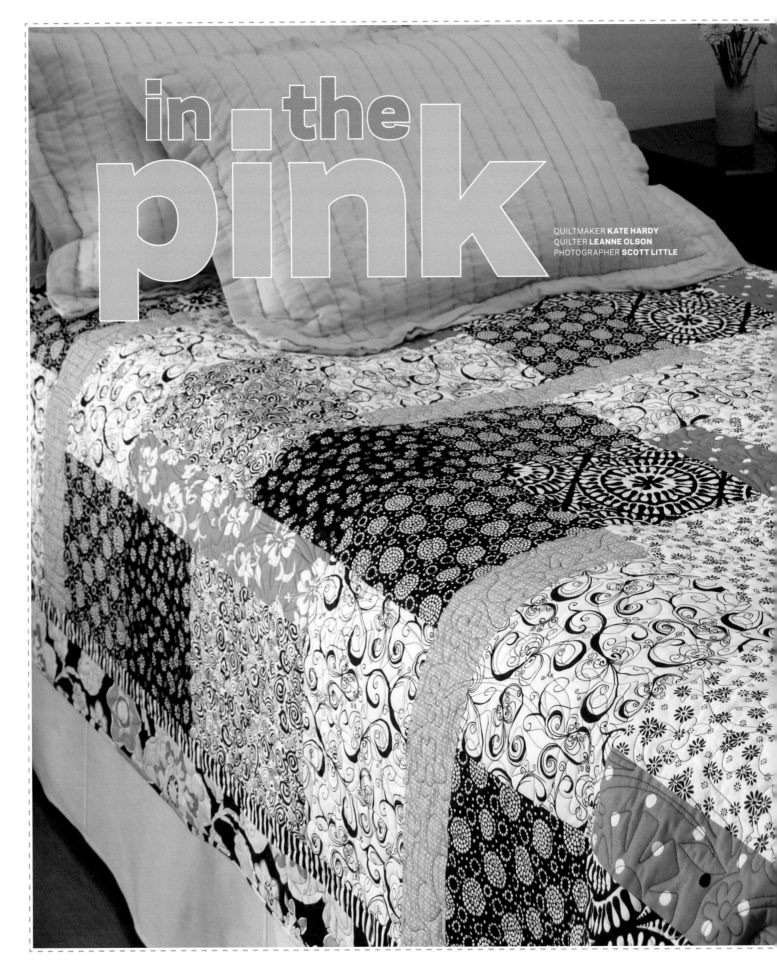

in the pink

QUILTMAKER **KATE HARDY**
QUILTER **LEANNE OLSON**
PHOTOGRAPHER **SCOTT LITTLE**

materials

- ▸ 1½ yards *total* assorted black-and-white prints (blocks)
- ▸ 2¼ yards *total* assorted white-and-black prints (blocks)
- ▸ ¾ yard *total* assorted pink prints (blocks)
- ▸ ½ yard black-and-white stripe (inner border)
- ▸ 1⅝ yards multicolor floral (outer border, binding)
- ▸ 3¾ yards backing fabric
- ▸ 72×91" batting

Finished quilt: 65½×84½"
Finished block: 19" square

Quantities are for 44/45"-wide, 100% cotton fabrics.
Measurements include ¼" seam allowances. Sew with right sides together unless otherwise stated.

cut fabrics

Cut pieces in the following order.

From assorted black-and-white prints, cut:
- ▸ 24—8½" squares (12 sets of 2 matching pieces)

From assorted white-and-black prints, cut:
- ▸ 24—8½×11½" rectangles (12 sets of 2 matching pieces)

From assorted pink prints, cut:
- ▸ 12—3½×19½" rectangles

From black-and-white stripe, cut:
- ▸ 7—1½×42" strips for inner border

From multicolor floral cut:
- ▸ 8—3½×42" strips for outer border
- ▸ 8—2½×42" binding strips

Giant blocks, each created from just five large pieces, make this zesty quilt a snap to complete.

assemble blocks

[**1**] Lay out two matching black-and-white print squares, two matching white-and-black print rectangles, and one pink print rectangle (**Block Assembly Diagram**).

[**2**] Sew together pieces in sections. Join sections to make a block. Press seams in one direction. The block should be 19½" square including seam allowances.

[**3**] Repeat steps 1 and 2 to make 12 blocks total.

assemble quilt center

[**1**] Referring to **Quilt Assembly Diagram** for placement, lay out blocks in rows.

[**2**] Sew together blocks in each row. Press seams in one direction, alternating direction with each row. Join rows to make quilt center. Press seams in one direction. The quilt center should be 57½×76½" including seam allowances.

add borders

[**1**] Cut and piece black-and-white stripe 1½×42" strips to make:
▸ 2—1½×76½" inner border strips
▸ 2—1½×59½" inner border strips

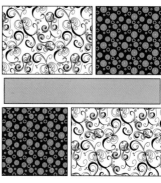

BLOCK ASSEMBLY DIAGRAM

[**2**] Sew long inner border strips to long edges of quilt center. Join short inner border strips to remaining edges. Press all seams toward inner border.

[**3**] Cut and piece multicolor floral 3½×42" strips to make:
▸ 2—3½×78½" outer border strips
▸ 2—3½×65½" outer border strips

QUILT ASSEMBLY DIAGRAM

[4] Add long outer border strips to long edges of quilt center. Join short outer border strips to remaining edges to complete quilt top. Press all seams toward outer border.

finish quilt

[1] Layer quilt top, batting, and backing; baste. (For details, see Complete the Quilt, *page 174*.)

[2] Quilt as desired. This quilt was stitched with an allover floral design.

[3] Bind with multicolor floral binding strips. (For details, see Complete the Quilt.)

»TIP«

If your ruler is slipping when you put pressure on it, adhere small sandpaper dots to the underside of the ruler. They're available at quilt shops, or you can make your own with a hole punch and fine-grain sandpaper.

quilting basics

Refer to these tips and techniques whenever you need
information for your projects.

make and use templates

To make templates, use easy-to-cut transparent template plastic, available at crafts supply stores.

To make a template, lay the plastic over a printed pattern. Trace the pattern using a permanent marker (and ruler for straight lines). Mark template with quilt name, letter, and any marked matching points (**Photo 1**).

For appliqué and hand piecing, the solid lines indicate finished size, and you will add any needed seams as instructed in project.

For machine piecing, the solid lines are cutting lines and dashed lines are seam lines. (An arrow on a pattern indicates the direction the fabric grain should run.)

Cut out the template and check it against the original pattern for accuracy (**Photo 2**). If it isn't accurate, the error (even if small) will multiply as you assemble a quilt.

Using a pushpin, make a hole in the template at all marked matching points (**Photo 3**). The hole must be large enough to accommodate a pencil point.

To trace the template on fabric, use a pencil, white dressmaker's pencil, chalk, or a special fabric marker that makes a thin, accurate line. Don't use a ballpoint or ink pen, which may bleed. Test all

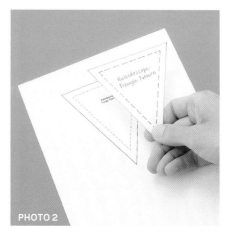

PHOTO 1

PHOTO 2

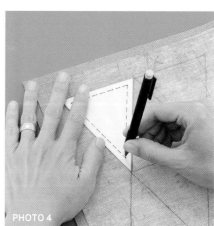

PHOTO 3

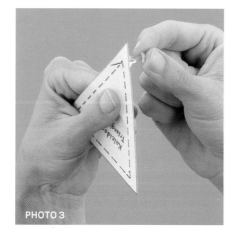

PHOTO 4

marking tools on a fabric scrap before using them. Place your fabric right side down on 220-grit sandpaper to prevent the fabric from stretching as you trace. Place the template facedown on the wrong side of the fabric with the template's grain line

parallel to the fabric's lengthwise or crosswise grain. Trace around the template. Mark any matching points through the holes in the template (**Photo 4**). (When sewing pieces together, line up and pin through matching points to ensure accurate assembly.)

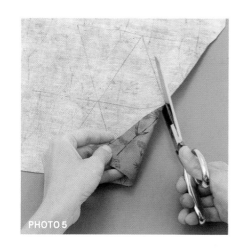

PHOTO 5

A template is a pattern made from extra-sturdy material so you can trace around it many times without wearing away the edges.

Repeat to trace the number of pieces needed, positioning the tracings without space between them. Use scissors or a rotary cutter and ruler to precisely cut fabric pieces on the drawn lines (**Photo 5**).

piece and appliqué

stitching: Quilting depends upon accuracy at every step. Use exact ¼" seam allowances throughout a quilt's construction. It isn't necessary to backstitch at the beginning of any seam that will be intersected by another seam later in the quiltmaking process. Use a stitch length of 10 to 12 stitches per inch (2.0- to 2.5-mm setting) to prevent stitches from unraveling before they're stitched over again. Secure seams that won't be sewn across again (such as those in borders) with a few backstitches.

pinning: When you want seam lines to line up perfectly, first match up seams of pieced units. Place an extra-fine pin diagonally through the pieces, catching both seam allowances. Avoid sewing over pins, as this can cause damage to your machine and injury to you.

pressing: Pressing seams ensures accurate piecing. Set the seam first by pressing it as it was sewn, without opening up the fabric pieces. This helps sink the stitches into the fabric, leaving you with a less bulky seam allowance.

The direction you press is important and is usually specified in the instructions. Usually, you will press the entire seam to one side rather than open. When two seams will be joined, first press the seams in opposite directions; this helps line up the seams perfectly and reduces bulk.

Press seam allowances in each row in opposite directions so they abut when rows are joined.

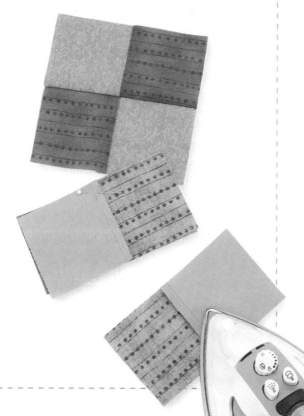

Make sure you are pressing, not ironing. Ironing means moving the iron while it is in contact with the fabric; this stretches and distorts seams. Pressing is lifting the iron off the surface of the fabric and putting it back down in another location.

machine appliqué: Many fast-and-easy appliqué projects are meant to be fused, then secured with stitching. Follow the directions in the project instructions for how to prepare appliqué pieces for fusing.

Pivoting outside curves. When appliquéing, position the presser foot so the left swing of the needle is on the appliqué and the right swing of the needle is just on the outer edge of the appliqué, grazing the foundation (**Photo 6**).

Stop at the first pivot point with the needle down in the fabric on the right-hand swing of the needle (see first red dot in **Diagram 1**; the arrow indicates the stitching direction). Raise the presser foot, pivot the fabric slightly, and begin stitching to the next pivot point. Repeat as needed to round the entire outer curve.

To help you know when to pivot, mark the edges of circular or oval appliqué pieces with the hours of

PHOTO 6

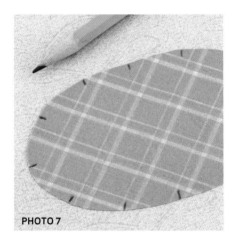

PHOTO 7

a clock; pivot the fabric at each mark (**Photo 7**).

Turning outside corners. When turning a corner, knowing where and when to stop and pivot makes a big difference in the finished look of your appliqué stitches.

Stop with the needle down in the fabric on the right-hand swing of the needle (see red dot in **Diagram 2**). Raise the presser foot and pivot the fabric. Lower the presser foot and begin stitching to the next edge (**Diagram 3**).

hand appliqué: To make a project portable, substitute hand appliqué for fusible appliqué. Use a sharp, between, straw, or milliners needle and the finest thread you can find that matches the appliqué pieces. Follow the directions in the project instructions for how to use freezer paper for cutting appliqué shapes.

Slip-stitch the edges. Pin or baste the appliqué to the appliqué foundation. Thread a handsewing needle with 18" of thread. Slip-stitch

DIAGRAM 1

DIAGRAM 2

DIAGRAM 3

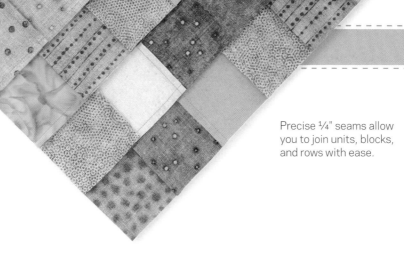

Precise ¼" seams allow you to join units, blocks, and rows with ease.

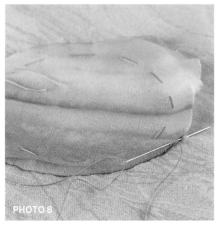

PHOTO 8

the appliqué edge in place by passing the needle through the folded edge of the appliqué and then through the appliqué foundation (**Photo 8**).

> ### »TIP«
>
> If you're having difficulty aligning seams when sewing rows together, try sewing with the seam allowance on top facing away from you as you guide the rows under the presser foot. This forces the top seam to butt up to the lower seam so the two automatically lock together.

Continue around the appliqué, taking smaller stitches around inside corners and curves.

Finish it up. End the thread by knotting it on the wrong side of the foundation, beneath the appliqué piece. Once all pieces have been appliquéd, place the foundation facedown on a terry cloth towel and press from the wrong side to prevent flattening the appliqués.

mitering borders

To add a border with mitered corners, first pin a border strip to a quilt top edge, matching the center of the strip and the center of the quilt top edge. Sew together, beginning and ending the seam ¼" from the quilt top corners (**Diagram 4**). Allow excess border fabric to extend beyond the edges. Repeat with the remaining border strips. Press the seam allowances toward the border strips.

At one corner, lap one border strip over the other (**Diagram 5**). Align the edge of a 90° right triangle with the raw edge of the top strip so the long edge of the triangle intersects the border seam in the corner. With a pencil, draw along the edge of the triangle from the seam out to the raw edge. Place the bottom border strip on top and

repeat the marking process.

With right sides together, match the marked seam lines and pin (**Diagram 6**).

Beginning with a backstitch at the inside corner, sew together the strips, stitching exactly on the marked lines. Check the right side to see that the corner lies flat. Trim the excess fabric, leaving a ¼" seam allowance. Press the seam open. Mark and sew the remaining corners in the same manner.

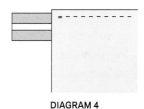

DIAGRAM 4

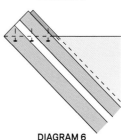

DIAGRAM 5

DIAGRAM 6

PHOTO 9

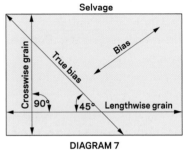

Selvage

Crosswise grain

True bias

Bias

90° 45° Lengthwise grain

DIAGRAM 7

cutting bias strips

Begin with a fabric square or rectangle. Using an acrylic ruler and rotary cutter, cut one edge at a 45° angle. Measure the desired width from the cut edge, then make a cut parallel to the edge (Photo 9). Repeat until you have the desired number of strips. Handle bias strips carefully to avoid distorting the fabric.

cutting on the bias

Bias runs diagonally between the lengthwise or crosswise grain line of a woven fabric. The "true" bias runs exactly at a 45° angle to the grain lines (Diagram 7) and has the most stretch in a woven fabric.

Because of their built-in stretch, strips cut on the bias can be easily curved or shaped. Use them when binding curved edges or to make curved appliqué pieces like vines or stems.

You can also cut directional fabrics like plaids or stripes on the bias for purely visual reasons. A bias binding cut from a stripe fabric creates a barber pole effect.

complete the quilt

choose your batting: Batting comes in different fibers (cotton, polyester, wool, and silk), and its loft can range greatly—from ⅛" to 1" or more. Generally, choose a low to medium loft for hand or machine quilting and a high loft for tied quilts. Pay attention to the manufacturer's label, which recommends the maximum distance between rows of quilting. If you exceed this distance, the batting will shift and bunch later, resulting in a lumpy quilt.

>> TIP <<

Keep needles for hand-stitching in good condition by wiping the surface after use and storing them in the original packaging.

Double-layer binding is easy to apply and adds durability to your finished quilt.

PHOTO 10

Place binding strips perpendicular to each other and stitch. Trim and press seams open to reduce bulk.

assemble the layers: Cut and piece the backing fabric to measure at least 3" bigger on all sides than the quilt top. Press seams open. Place the quilt backing wrong side up on a large, flat surface. Center and smooth the batting in place atop the quilt backing. Center the quilt top right side up on top of the batting and smooth out any wrinkles. Use safety pins or long hand stitches to baste all the layers together.

trim quilt: Trim the batting and backing fabric even with the quilt top edges; machine-baste a scant ¼" from quilt top edges if desired. (Some quilters prefer to wait until they have machine-sewn the binding to the quilt top before trimming the batting and backing.)

quilt as desired: A few of the more common machine-quilting methods follow.

Stitching in the ditch. Stitch just inside a seam line; the stitches should almost disappear into the seam. Using a walking foot attachment on your sewing machine will help prevent the quilt layers from shifting.

Stipple quilting. This random, allover stitching provides texture and interest behind a pattern. Use a darning foot and lower the feed dogs on your machine.

Outline quilting. Stitch ¼" from a seam line or the edge of an appliqué shape, just past the extra thickness of the seam allowance.

better binding

cut the strips: The cutting instructions for each project tell you the width and how many binding strips to cut. Unless otherwise specified, cut binding strips on the straight grain of the fabric. Join the binding strips with diagonal seams (**Photo 10**) to make one long binding strip. Trim seams to ¼" and press open.

To baste layers together, work from the center of the quilt out. Pin or stitch, spacing the pins or stitches 3" to 4" apart.

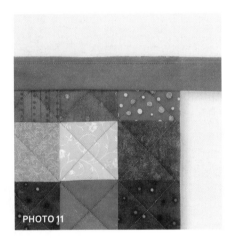

PHOTO 11

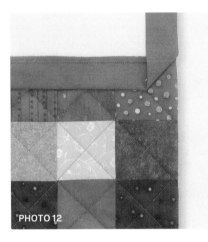

PHOTO 12

PHOTO 13

attach the binding: With the wrong side inside, fold under 1" at one end of the binding strip and press. Then fold the strip in half lengthwise with the wrong side inside. Place the binding strip against the right side of the quilt

»TIP«

If your quilting is more than 1" from the outer edges, baste the layers together around the quilt ⅜" from the edges. This will prevent the outside edges from ruffling and stretching as the binding is applied.

top along one edge, aligning the binding strip's raw edges with the quilt top's raw edge (do not start at a corner). Begin sewing the binding in place 2" from the folded end.

turn the corner: Stop sewing when you're ¼" from the corner (or a distance equal to the seam allowance you're using). Backstitch, then clip the threads (**Photo 11**). Remove the quilt from under the sewing-machine presser foot. Fold the binding strip upward, creating a diagonal fold, and finger-press (**Photo 12**). Holding the diagonal fold in place with your finger, bring the binding strip down in line with the next edge, making a horizontal fold that aligns with the quilt edge. Start sewing again at the top of the horizontal fold, stitching through all layers (**Photo 13**).

Sew around the quilt, turning each corner in the same manner.

finish it up: When you return to the starting point, encase the binding strip's raw edge inside the folded end and finish sewing to the starting point. Trim the batting and backing fabric even with the quilt top edges if not done earlier.

Turn the binding over the edge to the back. Hand-stitch the binding to the backing fabric only, covering any machine stitching. To make the binding corners on the quilt back match the mitered corners on the quilt front, hand-stitch up to a corner and make a fold in the binding. Secure the fold with a couple of stitches, then continue stitching the binding in place along the next edge.